Managing the Curriculum for Children with Severe Motor Difficulties

A Practical Approach

Pilla A.C. Pickles

David Fulton Publishers

London

David Fulton Publishers Ltd
Ormond House, 26–27 Boswell Street, London WC1N 3JD

First published in Great Britain by David Fulton Publishers 1998

Note: The right of the author to be identified as the author of this work
has been asserted by her in accordance with the Copyright, Designs and
Patents Act 1988.

Copyright © Pilla A.C. Pickles 1998

British Library Cataloguing in Publication Data

A catalogue record for this book is available from the British Library

ISBN 1–85346–511–9

Typeset by FSH Print & Production Ltd.
Printed by Bell and Bain Ltd, Glasgow

Contents

Acknowledgements

I would like to thank the many children, parents, friends and colleagues who have been my inspiration in writing this book. In particular I would like to thank the staff, children and families of Elmgrove First School in Harrow for their kindness and support over the years; and the staff, parents and pupils in Barnet mainstream and special schools. Without them, this book would not have been possible.

I would also like to thank the following individuals for their constructive criticism and advice on the book in draft form: Barbara Beverly (Support Assistant, Barnet); Denise Cawthorne (Head teacher, Harrow); Eileen Clark (retired teacher, Harrow); Elizabeth Clery (Advisory Teacher – Visual Impairment, Harrow); Caroline Cogan (SENCO, Harrow) Liz Cowne (Education Consultant); Liz Creamer (Chief Paediatric Occupational Therapy, Harrow) Alison Jones (teacher, Harrow); Angie Lawrence (SENCO, SEN Governor, Harrow); Hilary Lucas (Education Consultant); Bridget Morrison (friend and supporter); Sharon Raphael (Physical and Advisory Teacher, Barnet); Henrietta Singleton (Support Assistant, Barnet); Valerie Standen (Manager Specialist Provision, Barnet) Grania Usher (Educational Psychologist, Harrow/Barnet); Tanya Zucker (Preschool Home Teacher, Barnet).

Most of all I would like to thank my two sons, Ben for drawing the graphics and Tim for his advice on computing, and my dear husband, John, for all his love and support over the years.

Foreword

Children with severe physical disabilities were, for many decades, placed in special schools. In the last decade or so, since the 1981 Education Act, more and more parents and LEAs have been choosing a mainstream placement for these children with complex needs.

The recent Green Paper proposes an even more consistent drive for inclusive education. To give youngsters with physical needs full access to the whole curriculum and the life of the mainstream school in a meaningful way is quite challenging for schools and teachers.

The author of this book, Pilla Pickles, met this challenge herself when she ran an integrated resource for children with physical disabilities in the London Borough of Harrow. She used her previous special education experience to work with parents, therapists and teachers, building a team to support the children. Now, she coordinates physical support for the London Borough of Barnet to meet the same challenge in a large number of schools.

Initially, it was my privilege to support Pilla and help solve the many problems such a resource poses in its first years. Since then I have continued to admire Pilla's positive and often ingenious approach to meeting each and every challenge. Her goal is always to use the most easily available resource to bring out the potential strengths in each child.

This book is the outcome of a life's work in special needs. It will become an essential source of support to all, be they teacher, therapist, support assistant or parent, who want to know how to find practical solutions to the everyday challenge of providing a full, but inclusive, curriculum for pupils with complex needs.

Elizabeth Cowne
Open University Tutor
Educational Consultant

How to use this book

It is more likely that this book will be dipped into rather than read from cover to cover. For this reason it has been necessary to repeat the need for close liaison and involvement with therapists and the support team in every chapter and to emphasise the need for good record-keeping.

Catalogue supplies and other information relevant to each chapter can be found in the Appendix with the same number, e.g. equipment mentioned in chapter 4 will have details in Appendix 4. Full names, addresses and contact details are in Appendix 14 and further useful addresses are given in Appendix 15.

The aim of this book is to provide practical guidance and advice to all schools in managing the curriculum for pupils with severe motor difficulties and in working in a multi-agency support team. It takes schools through the processes required to set up successful inclusion and is especially useful for mainstream schools with little or no experience in dealing with such complex pupils. The multi-sensory approach, activities and differentiation techniques used in this book are appropriate for pupils with severe motor difficulties, but are equally suitable for all. They are just another way of accessing the curriculum for all children.

Chapter 1 Towards inclusion

This chapter gives a brief, historical picture of disabilities in education and defines disability, handicap, integration and inclusion. It looks at changes in attitudes in education and society and the recent positive move towards inclusion in the Green Paper of October 1997 (DfEE 1997). It emphasises that a commitment to inclusion also requires a commitment to funding and training.

Chapter 2 Working as a team

This chapter defines the support team as those professionals working with the child on a regular basis. It lists, and briefly describes, the role of each member of the team including parents and professionals in Education, Health and Social Services.

Chapter 3 School planning to meet the needs

This chapter describes the need for careful planning and liaison with the support team. It provides lists of questions about transport, mobility, specialist equipment and therapy and also questions to be asked when interviewing assistants to work with children with severe motor difficulties. It describes the importance of establishing all the child's needs and the need for disability awareness training for the whole staff.

Part One
Working as a team
setting up support

Chapter 4 Organising timetables, equipment and procedures

This chapter is about planning the timetable and the Individual Education Plan (IEP). It discusses issues about equipment and lists the main equipment likely to be used by a child with severe motor difficulties in school. It also discusses storage of equipment, toileting, health and hygiene.

Chapter 5 Time management

This chapter is about time management and the difficulties of working in a large team. It describes the role of the key worker and gives some useful liaison ideas for school staff and members of the support team. It describes the primary support liaison folder and the secondary school passport, which enable the support team to communicate and keep up to date with each other's work, while giving the pupil the confidence that their needs will be understood.

Part Two
Practical ideas
to access the
curriculum

Chapter 6 Including therapies in the curriculum

This chapter highlights the importance of partnership between different services working together as one team and discusses how different therapies can be included in the curriculum. It describes and lists common therapy targets, their effects on the child, and activities which can be incorporated into the curriculum to develop further skills and independence.

Chapter 7 Practical ideas to introduce therapy into activities

This chapter explains how, by using simple everyday objects, activities can be modified to cover therapy and educational targets. It describes how to adapt flash cards and games for greater ease of access and how to devise games to cover education and therapy.

Chapter 8 Computers and technology

This chapter looks at different technology and gives advice on what to look for when choosing a computer and software. It describes and lists different peripherals and the importance of involving the occupational therapist for seating and positioning. For many pupils, technology will be their main means of recording.

Chapter 9 Accessing the curriculum with pen/cil and paper

This chapter describes the need to work with the occupational therapist to devise ways of accessing the curriculum with pen/cil and paper, as well as the use of technology. It explains the need for a carefully devised programme to ensure the child progresses from one stage to the next and how lines, dots and scribbles can record the curriculum through the use of multiple choice. It carefully describes how the child can learn to draw lines at different angles and how these can be used for recording.

Chapter 10 Reading. If I can read I can ...

This chapter emphasises the importance of reading and gives specific guidance on devising a reading programme to meet individual needs. It describes the difficulties faced by some pupils with severe motor difficulties and the need to create ways to consolidate learning. It gives lots of clear, practical games and activities to help pupils with poor fine motor skills to learn to read, using pencil and paper and technology.

Chapter 11 Maths and science – will my chair fit in your lunchbox?

This chapter discusses the difficulties in mathematical and science concepts faced by many children with severe motor difficulties and gives practical ideas and strategies to help. It lists useful equipment and practical games to help learn and assess concepts.

Chapter 12 Physical education, technology and geography

This chapter lists questions to ask the support team about individual pupils to ensure that physical activities are appropriate, discusses ways of working and lists ideas and games to be incorporated in the PE curriculum. There is a list of technology equipment likely to be useful and ideas and equipment useful for Geography.

Chapter 13 Music and art

This chapter gives practical ideas and advice on accessing the Music curriculum and lists useful instruments and games, including the use of technology. In Art, it highlights the importance of the process of exploring different mediums, rather than focusing on the end result. There are also art ideas, accessible to all children, which have equal results for disabled and able-bodied pupils and ideas on different ways pupils, who cannot draw themselves, can illustrate their work.

Part One

Working as a team setting up support

Chapter 1

Towards inclusion

This book is about accessing the curriculum for children with severe motor difficulties affecting some or all of their limbs. Limited hand function, fine motor difficulties, and speech problems may also affect the child. Severe motor difficulties may have been diagnosed at birth, at about the age of two or at a later date, and deteriorating conditions such as muscular dystrophy or Friedreich's ataxia may not be diagnosed until the child attends school. Some children may have motor difficulties as a result of an accident or illness, which can happen at any time.

Every child is an individual and every child with motor difficulties is even more of an individual. Disability affects people in different ways and it is dangerous and impossible to predict the intellectual abilities, emotional needs, outcome of different physical disabilities, and the level of independence any child might attain. This book aims to create equality in the classroom by removing barriers to education and using the expertise of the wider support team including Health, Social Services, Education and parents. Adapting curriculum activities to meet the needs of the child with severe motor difficulties, as described in this book, enables full inclusion. As a multi-sensory approach *it is useful for all children*, but especially for teaching children with a wide variety of needs, and should be seen as just another approach to learning. The aim is to support the school and parents to meet the needs of the child and, in doing so, enable the child to grow into a confident, independent and valued member of society.

Disability or handicap?

Disability is sometimes incorrectly used synonymously with 'handicap'. Words and definitions are always changing and it is important to avoid using words which will offend. The Disability Movement, including the Royal Association for Disability and Rehabilitation (RADAR) presently agree to define 'disability' and 'handicap' in the following way.

- '*Disability* is the loss or limitation of opportunities to take part in the normal life of the community on an equal level with others, due to physical and social barriers.'
- '*Impairment* is the functional limitation within the individual caused by physical, mental or sensory impairment.' (Male 1997)

We have come a long way

Segregation of children and adults with physical disabilities has been going on for hundreds of years. In the late nineteenth century it was recognised that deaf and blind children had a right to education, but at the same time, children with physical disabilities were called 'defective'. It was believed that mental and physical defects were closely related and that a 'mental defect' could be diagnosed by physical signs. Children with difficulties in communication, movement or mobility and those who had fits were labelled 'defective', thought to be 'ineducable' and sent to the thousands of asylums and institutions for 'morons, idiots and imbeciles' around the country. They were thought to undermine the British nation and to increase poverty, physical degradation, crime and sexual immorality.

Historically, the medical profession had a lead role in determining the type of education for children with disabilities, or indeed whether they should be educated at all! The medical model saw the disability as the problem and the doctor's role was to cure and normalise the child. Doctors had real power in deciding what happened in the child's life and also later on, as an adult.

This situation improved substantially with the 1944 Education Act which made education available for 'pupils who suffer from any disability of mind or body, by providing either in special schools or otherwise, special educational treatment, that is to say education by special methods for persons suffering from that disability'. This was a positive move, but it segregated children with disabilities into a wide range of special schools, away from society and mainstream schools and often away from their families.

Over 50 years later the 1981 Education Act moved away from the power of the medics and the growing number of special schools. It focused on educational need and provision, introducing the multi-disciplinary assessment, resulting in a 'statement of educational need' which required joint decision-making between Social Services, Health and Education. It also recognised the value of parents in the assessment and their rights to participate in decisions about provision. The Act's basic principle was that all children should be educated and included in ordinary schools, wherever possible.

What is integration and what is inclusion?

Integration is sometimes incorrectly used synonymously with inclusion. The Warnock Report (DES 1978) described integration of children with Special Educational Needs (SEN) in mainstream schools as locational, social or functional. The term 'integration' is illustrated in *Altogether Better* by Micheline Mason and Richard Rieser in their excellent book and video raising awareness about disabilities. They describe integration as:

* Geographical integration: Disabled children may be educated in units or schools on the same campus or site as their non-disabled peers, but not mix, even socially.
* Periodic integration: Children from special schools are bussed in to a mainstream school at a regular time each week for 'integration'. Or an 'integration event' is organised.
* Social integration: Disabled children may share meals, playtime and assemblies together, but not be taught together.
* Functional integration: Disabled and non-disabled children are taught in the same class.

It must be remembered, however, that inclusion is not another term for functional integration. Functional integration allows the possibility of inclusion, but does not, itself, achieve it.

Inclusion is a process which recognises that impairment and disability are common to all and values the individual as a person, enabling access, equality and achievement. It is about a whole-school policy where the community accepts and values diversity.

A few years ago education supported anti-racism and anti-sexism. Most schools now welcome visitors in many languages and books and posters reflect the positive images of ethnic minorities and females. It is now time for people with disabilities to be seen in the same positive light and to be included as part of society at every level. Young children, growing up in an inclusive school environment where diversity is valued, are the parents and employers of tomorrow. It will be their attitude, and philosophies that will make positive changes in society to develop an inclusive society and environment. This book is about building and working in a multi-professional support team to ensure that everything possible is done to help the school overcome barriers to inclusion, to enable the child to become as independent as possible and to ensure the child is valued as a person in society.

In 1992 two reports *Getting in on the Act* and *Getting the Act Together* (Audit Commission/HMI 1992a and b) reviewed the ways Local Education Authorities (LEAs) met the objectives of the 1981 Act. They identified that two-fifths of parents wanted their children to be educated in mainstream rather than in special schools, if the schools had the support and financial resources. The reports identified that LEAs were failing to implement the 1981 Education Act and that sufficient resources and training had not been provided. Unfortunately the 1993 Act (DfE 1993) again, did not address the issue of funding and central resources. There was no additional money and with scarce resources, adaptations to school buildings, already desperately in need of repair, were extremely costly. The majority of our schools were built for able-bodied children in the last hundred years, when society created environments in order to exclude, rather than include people with disabilities. Access to schools and the environment is crucial for the successful inclusion of people with disabilities. A strong commitment to inclusion goes hand in hand with a commitment to funding. The best philosophy in the world cannot enable a person in a wheelchair to negotiate a flight of steep steps.

Changing attitudes – towards inclusion

The Green Paper followed the White Paper 'Excellence in Schools' (The Stationery Office 1997) which committed the government to raising standards in all schools. The Green Paper has an inclusive vision encompassing children with Special Educational Needs (SEN) and appears to be a significant move towards the inclusion of the majority of children with SEN into mainstream schools. In the Foreword, written by the Secretary of State for Education and Employment, the Rt Hon David Blunkett said:

The Green Paper – Excellence for all children – October 1997

> The great majority of children with SEN will, as adults, contribute economically; all will contribute as members of society. Schools have to prepare all children for these roles. That is a strong reason for educating children with SEN, as far as possible, with their peers. Where all children are included as equal partners in the school community, the benefits are felt by all. That is why we are committed to comprehensive and enforceable civil rights for disabled people. Our aspirations as a nation must be for all our people.

3

A more positive climate for disabilities

The Green Paper (DfEE 1997: 9 and 10) states that by the year 2002 the government aims to achieve:

- A growing number of mainstream schools, willing and able to accept children with a range of special educational needs: as a consequence, an increasing proportion of those children with statements of SEN who would currently be placed in special schools will be educated in mainstream schools.
- National and local programmes will be in place to support increased inclusion.
- Special and mainstream schools will be working alongside and in support of one another.
- Regional planning machinery for SEN will be in place across England, helping to coordinate provision for low-incidence disabilities, specialist teacher training and other aspects of SEN.
- There will be a clear structure for teachers' professional development in SEN, from a strengthened attention to SEN issues in initial training through to improved training to head teachers, SEN coordinators and other SEN specialists.
- There will be a national framework for training learning support assistants.
- There will be improved cooperation and coordination between local authorities, social services departments and health authorities, with the focus on meeting children's special needs more effectively.
- Speech and language therapy will be provided more effectively for children who need it. We will consider whether any changes to the provision of speech therapy should be extended to cover the arrangements for the funding of physiotherapy and occupational therapy and whether ... the provision of school nurses would benefit from better collaboration.
- The Department will be collecting information about the experiences, once they have left school, of young people with SEN, to help schools and colleges prepare young people for adult life more effectively.

Mainstream and special schools working together

There are large numbers of children with disabilities and severe motor difficulties included in mainstream schools today. Many teachers and schools have had little or no experience of teaching such complex children and will need specialist training and support. Linking and using the expertise of staff in special schools is a valuable way forward. However, it must be remembered that educating a pupil with severe and complex needs in a special school, with six or seven pupils in one class, is a very different scenario from teaching pupils in a busy mainstream school with thirty or more in the class. It is dangerous to assume that special school staff are the 'experts' and 'will be a source of training and advice to mainstream colleagues'. (DfEE 1997). It is important to understand that both sets of staff are 'experts' in different ways and the need is to learn from each other and to work together. Recent inclusion of pupils with physical disabilities has meant that special schools are now catering for pupils with more severe and complex needs, although staff levels may not have changed significantly and extra training has not always been available.

Historically, therapists have worked in special schools for children with physical disabilities and many followed the medical model by focusing on the individual and their impairment and seeing the disability as the problem. Finding a cure and normalising the impairment was seen as the priority and the educational, emotional and social needs of the individual were secondary. Thankfully it seems we are now on a roller coaster which has chugged up the hills and is gathering speed down the other side. The needs of the whole child are now assessed and better met. The Disability Movement has been campaigning to change society's views for many years and positive changes are at last happening. Society is moving faster and faster towards inclusion, though it still has a long way to go!

Therapy in special and mainstream schools

A full understanding of therapy, combined with good liaison and training, is vital for schools, parents and carers. Therapy should be seen as part of everyday living and the responsibility of the whole support team. Without understanding, the danger is that therapy will be seen as something to be 'done' to the child by therapists 'to make things better'. It may be seen as Health's responsibility and educationalists may feel that it is not their responsibility at all. Therapy programmes depend entirely on the child's medical and health needs and require continual assessment by doctors and therapists. Good liaison between teachers and therapists results in teachers' understanding of therapeutic needs, so that therapy can be included in the curriculum, handling of the child and daily living. Teachers are able to learn from other professionals, and new skills acquired are useful for many other children. In this way teachers, alongside the wider support team, can use their educational expertise to plan the curriculum, including therapeutic and educational targets, and teach strategies to enable the child to gain independence and success.

Therapy is Health and Education's responsibility

In the past, the move to include children with severe motor difficulties and other special needs in mainstream schools has been positive, but has not been coordinated; there has been insufficient access, funding and training to allow it to work. Successful schools following a policy of inclusion and equality have worked mainly as a result of the dedication of individuals in schools, Health Services and LEAs. Health and LEAs need an overall, long-term plan of support, training and funding, if inclusion of children with severe motor difficulties into mainstream schools is to succeed. The wheelchair and sticks may be seen as the difficulty and the belief is that providing space and access is the only answer. Teachers need the support of a multi-professional team to understand the medical and therapeutic needs and to be able to plan the curriculum for pupils with possibly complex, hidden handicaps. Good practice is for one single achievable IEP covering all of the child's needs.

Support and training between Health and Education

Chapter 2

Working as a team

For the purposes of this book I will refer to the *support team* as those professionals working with the child on a regular, hands-on basis and the *support network* as the team, including the additional professionals, who are involved less frequently.

In the preschool years the child with severe motor difficulties and its family has the support of a network of professionals from Health, Social Services, the Early Years Education Team and peripatetic teachers for vision and hearing. It can be difficult for schools to understand that sometimes up to 30 professionals may have worked with the child in the first five years. Schools dealing with a child with severe motor difficulties for the first time will have had no experience or understanding of the demands placed on parents and families by this large network of supporters.

Parent partnership

Under the Children Act (DHSS 1989) parents are defined as those who have parental responsibility for the child or who have full care. The value of parent partnership has long been debated since the 1970 Handicapped Children Act (DES 1970), when parents began to push for change in the education system. Over the years legislation has increased parents' rights. The 1993 Education Act (DfE 1993) introduced new inspection procedures (OFSTED) with parents being invited to meet the inspectors and raise any issues about the school. The SEN Tribunal gives parents the right to appeal against LEA decisions. The introduction of the Code of Practice (DfE 1994a) emphasised the importance of involving parents and the 1997 Green Paper (DfEE 1997) continues to push for parent partnership.

Parents should have information on the school's SEN policy, on the support available for pupils with SEN in the school, and be involved in assessment and decision-making, including their child's IEP. They need to be aware of their rights and fully understand the five-staged assessment procedure and any LEA services which might be able to support their child. The initial shock of a child's diagnosis is devastating and parents and family members often feel seesawing emotions of guilt and fear. It may take years to come to terms with the diagnosis, if at all, and is a lonely time. Parents and families need support to share their emotions and anxieties and to help them plan for the future. Their lives become an endless round of hospital visits to various doctors, consultants and paediatricians, physiotherapists, occupational and speech and language therapists. Dealing with such vulnerable parents takes time, effort and understanding to make them feel confident that the school can meet the needs of their child. It is important to make time to talk and involve parents through a home liaison book, regular meetings or by telephone. Partnership involves listening to other's opinions and making decisions with give-and-take on both sides.

In the child's early years some parents may have moved towards specific medical treatments, such as conductive education, which they believe is right for their child. It is important to understand and acknowledge parents' wishes and beliefs in the treatment of their child, even if it does not coincide with the school's. Careless words can shatter illusions and set the foundation for a poor, one-sided partnership. Schools need to work together with parents, therapists and doctors to ensure that the individual needs of pupils are fully understood and met, wherever possible. It is inevitable that there will be times when compromises have to be made, but as part of the support team, parents must be involved in any decisions affecting their child. Parents are the real key players in the game, knowing the child best of all, but the strains and stresses on parents of children with SEN, in particular children with severe motor difficulties, who often need 24-hour care, must not be underestimated. The needs of the parents and the child within the family should be seen as a whole.

Head teacher

The head teacher is appointed by the school governors and is responsible for the organisation and running of the school ensuring that school policies are written and reviewed in consultation with staff. Head teachers are likely to delegate most of the SEN work to the special needs coordinator (SENCO). It is important that the head teacher and members of the senior management team fully understand and prioritise the importance of therapy, specialist equipment, liaison and the input from all members of the support team and parents.

Special needs coordinator (SENCO)

The SENCO has a pivotal role in the successful integration of pupils with special needs. According to the Code of Practice (DfE 1994a) the SENCO's role is to:

* manage the day to day running of the school's SEN policy
* liaise with and advise teaching staff
* coordinate provision for pupils with SEN
* maintain the SEN register and oversee the records for SEN pupils
* liaise with parents
* contribute to in-service training
* liaise with external agencies, including the educational psychology, medical and social services and voluntary bodies.

Many head teachers delegate management of support staff, organisation of staged assessment and annual reviews and the writing and collating of evidence for stage 4 multi-professional assessments to the SENCO. Many SENCOs also have teaching commitments and their very complex role can become unmanageable.

It is more effective if the SENCO belongs to the senior management team and special needs is shared with a team of teachers. No one should be torn between the huge amount of paperwork of a coordinator's role, time to support pupils, parents and colleagues,

School-based support

liaison time with members of the wider support team and time for their own teaching commitments. Each school develops its own SEN policy and its own ways of managing SEN within the school.

Although SENCOs are vital to a successful school SEN policy, they must not be thought of as the only support. All class teachers are responsible for meeting the needs of the pupils in their class, referring to others for advice. Every teacher in the school must take a share of responsibility for pupils with SEN and the school needs the support and backing of the wider support team to feel confident in meeting individual pupils' needs.

Class teacher

At the end of the day it is the class teacher who, as an expert in education, plans, delivers and ensures access to the curriculum, liaising with support staff and the SENCO. Teaching a child with severe motor difficulties is complex. Most teachers have had no training in teaching children with disabilities and success is dependent on how well the support team, via the SENCO, is able to support the teacher. School management needs to plan carefully to ensure that classes are not overloaded.

Support assistant

The role of the assistant is crucial for the successful integration of children with severe motor difficulties, enabling their inclusion in all school activities, looking after their physical and medical needs, facilitating access to the curriculum and supporting the teacher to support the child. There were over 24,000 assistants working in schools across the country in 1997 and the effect of the Green Paper (DfEE 1997) will be to increase this number substantially in order to implement the policy of inclusion for children with SEN.

Assistants are usually managed by the SENCO, senior school staff or sometimes the class teacher. They should have clear guidelines, an up-to-date job description and a full understanding of school policies, with ongoing training by relevant staff in Health and Education. The support assistant's main aim should be to enable the pupil to become as independent as possible, allowing them time and space to achieve activities independently without being overprotective. It is a complex role, likely to involve carrying out physiotherapy, occupational therapy and possibly speech and language therapy programmes, under the guidance of the therapists. This is particularly so in mainstream schools where therapists visit regularly, but are not based on site. In many special schools, therapy is always carried out by therapists and assistants are not involved. There are benefits of having therapy carried out by support assistants given that there is ongoing training, advice and support from the appropriate therapists and good liaison with the teachers and school staff. Therapy programmes carried out by assistants and parents maintain the child at the same physical level, while therapists monitor and assess the child, planning and extending treatment.

All staff, including supply teachers, need to be aware of the support assistant's role and ensure that they are not overloaded with classroom tasks, especially if they support an individual statemented pupil. The assistant is there to support the teacher in supporting the child in whatever is the most suitable way for that teacher, lesson and child, but is not a general classroom assistant. Good teamwork and liaison leads to successful inclusion.

Support teacher

Many schools have additional teachers working in partnership with class teachers, providing extra teaching support for pupils. Support teachers in schools are not required to have specialist training, but may be experienced in teaching pupils with a wide range of special needs. They work in different ways, sometimes working alongside the class teacher, taking the whole class to allow the class teacher to work with specific pupils, or working with a group of pupils or an individual pupil in or out of the classroom. Each school has its own way of working, which it feels best meets the needs of the school and its pupils.

Preschool teacher

The first five years are crucial for education as well as for the medical and physical development of the child. Play is the foundation for learning and a child unable to explore the world due to their motor impairment often has difficulties understanding basic concepts especially in maths and science. Learning is part of play and play is part of learning. Advice to parents and families from a teacher in the early years helps parents understand the importance of play and different techniques, toys and equipment, which will facilitate play for the child with motor difficulties and therefore help learning.

Establishment of an early years team, including Health, Education and Social Services, builds firm foundations for the future. This multi-disciplinary team will write the advice for an assessment of the child's SEN, if required, and facilitate a move into an educational placement, supporting the child and the parents and advising staff.

Teachers of the deaf – (TODs)

These teachers have a qualification to teach pupils who have a mild to profound hearing loss, and are likely to be funded by the LEA and be centrally or school-based. Peripatetic teachers move around the borough advising and supporting schools and parents, working with children from birth to 19 years of age. The TOD trains and advises on classroom management, specific gives advice for individual pupils, advises on differentiation techniques and the use and care of hearing aids, and may organise and support signing for those pupils who need this to help them communicate. Some pupils may be allocated specific teaching support from a TOD and close liaison with the support team is crucial, particularly for pupils with motor difficulties who may have difficulties using signing. A hearing-impaired pupil may be advised to sit in the middle at the front of the class, but if they also have severe motor

Local authority based supports

difficulties, it is often necessary for them to sit elsewhere in class. It is important that the TOD, as part of the support team, advises the school from their own particular perspective, leaving the SENCO and class teacher to take ownership and agree on a solution. With this support the class teacher can plan the best seating position for each lesson.

Teachers for the visually impaired

These teachers have extra training and qualifications to teach pupils with a visual impairment and work in much the same way as the TOD, funded centrally by the LEA. Peripatetic teachers, work with pupils from birth to 19 years of age, giving advice and support in the home and schools. They advise and train schools on positioning, classroom management, specific guidance for individual pupils, and differentiation techniques. They advise staff on seating, position, size of print, clarity of presentation of materials, use of blackboard, and ways of accessing the curriculum including the use of technology, specific software to enlarge text and the use of Braille for blind children. Some pupils may be allocated specific teaching support from a teacher of the visually impaired. Close liaison with the support team is crucial, particularly for pupils with severe motor difficulties who may have difficulties with seating and positioning and may need specialist software, switches and peripherals.

Psychology service

Educational psychologists

Educational psychologists are funded by the LEA and based centrally, although some may work on a private basis. They are a professionally qualified and experienced teachers with a degree in psychology and a postgraduate qualification in educational psychology. They study the emotional, social, intellectual and physical development of children and young people, working closely with teachers and parents, and may advise on suitable programmes for children with learning difficulties or behaviour modification plans for dealing with children with behaviour difficulties. Some educational psychologists specialise in one particular area of need, such as hearing impairment or physical disabilities.

Visiting Health professionals

Physiotherapists

Physiotherapists are important members of the support team as it is only with their advice and support that children with severe motor difficulties can succeed in mainstream schools. Teachers do not have the skills or training to manage correctly the physical needs of these children and are reliant on the therapists for training, advice and guidance. Physiotherapists are employed and funded by Health, although many are now independent and funded privately by individuals. They may be based at hospitals, clinics or special schools and make visits to mainstream schools and homes to treat individual children, as well as working in specialist centres, aiming for as great a degree of independence as possible and maintaining and developing the individual's physical abilities.

Part of the physiotherapist's role is to train parents, carers and assistants to carry out physiotherapy exercises. There are huge benefits from this daily therapy, carried out by another adult, under the direction of the physiotherapist. Therapeutic aims are now better understood by more people, enabling them to be incorporated into daily living wherever possible. Standing, walking, eating, painting, reaching and sitting are all therapeutic if the child is positioned and handled correctly. Close liaison and training of parents, teachers and assistants by the physiotherapists, as members of the support team, ensures that correct handling, independence, positioning and seating is prioritised in class and in the home. Physiotherapists also advise on activities which can be included in the curriculum. They often work together with occupational therapists, especially with seating, positioning, fine motor skills and use of large and small equipment. They may advise on the lifting and handling of a specific child, but are not usually permitted to give general lifting and handling training. There are specially qualified therapists and instructors to teach lifting of children, adults and objects, and all schools require specialist training in this area. Physiotherapists' main responsibilities are to:

- liaise with paediatricians, hospital consultants, other therapists and centres;
- advise and assess the need for specialist equipment;
- devise physiotherapy programmes to meet the needs of the individual child;
- assess and advise on mobility aids, management of the child on stairs, slopes and ramps and mobility around the school and playground;
- manage and advise on the treatment of children with conditions needing chest therapy, such as cystic fibrosis;
- manage and advise on other deteriorating conditions such as muscular dystrophy.

It is very important for school staff to be aware of the therapeutic needs of the individual and for the physiotherapist, class teacher, assistant and SENCO or key worker to have time allocated to liaise.

Occupational therapists

The occupational therapist's training and skills are required to ensure that children with severe motor difficulties can be successfully included in mainstream schools. Occupational therapists are concerned with achieving optimum functional performance skills in all areas of life. Detailed assessment of motor, sensory, perceptual and social skills is a forerunner to the development of all life skills including dressing, eating, toileting and practical skills within the classroom and around the school. They may advise on specialist equipment and structural adaptations to allow independent or full access to the environment. They may provide remediation programmes for fine motor, sensory and perceptual difficulties in home and school. They also advise on solutions to practical problems as diverse as independent feeding, use of a computer or how to complete a scientific experiment. They advise on ·seating and positioning, length of time spent in any one position, and classroom management, which is crucial if children with severe motor difficulties are to have full access to the curriculum and reach their optimum potential in school.

Speech and language therapists

Speech and language therapists treat children with speech and language difficulties. They may work independently or be employed by Health and Education Services. They are usually based at hospitals, clinics, special schools or centres and make visits to mainstream schools and homes to assess, treat and monitor individual children. They diagnose speech and language difficulties and disorders and devise programmes to improve communication skills. These may be carried out by parents, teachers, assistants or the children themselves, at home or in school, under their direction. Some children have physical difficulties which affect their hearing, speech or voice production and therapists will assess and train the child in alternative means of communication, which might include the use of Makaton, Bliss symbolics, other symbol systems or a communication aid. They advise on eating problems and can help the child with chewing, biting, swallowing and strategies to overcome dribbling. Working together with the occupational therapist, they advise on eating, drinking and the use of equipment to enable the child with motor difficulties to become as independent as possible.

Therapists work with children who have a speech or language difficulty, but both teachers and therapists work with the development of language and their roles may overlap. It is important to have effective, timetabled liaison to establish good and efficient working practices in schools to:

- clarify and develop awareness of the roles of each member of the support team,
- share information and resources,
- monitor the child's use of language in a variety of different situations, and
- agree realistic goals and programmes to be carried out and reviewed.

School doctor and nurse

Some schools may have an allocated school doctor and a school nurse, although many health authorities no longer employ doctors in schools. The doctor is part of the support team and in some schools carries out medical examinations and sight and audiology screening tests, referring children to a hospital or paediatrician for further tests if concerned. The school doctor and nurse support and advise on medical and health issues, establishing medical procedures and organising training for a variety of medical topics such as epilepsy, asthma, headlice, emergency resuscitation and administering rectal diazepam. They support and advise schools on establishing emergency medical procedures for individuals, dealing with health and safety issues such as blood and bodily fluids and disposal of medical waste. They may help set up counselling for staff and parents, for example, when a pupil has a deteriorating condition or requires complicated treatment or surgery. It is likely that a child with severe motor difficulties will be treated by consultants and paediatricians in one or more hospitals. The school doctor can be a great support to parents and school ensuring that medical, therapeutic and health needs are met, and also act as a link to the rest of the medical network.

Community paediatrician

Children with severe motor difficulties will usually be referred to a community paediatrician by their general practitioner or may be seen at birth. Paediatricians are medical doctors who are trained specifically to work with children and are based in clinics or hospitals. Frequently, severe motor difficulties are not diagnosed until the child is a few months old and often not until the child is two years old. Difficulties may be picked up by the parents, the general practitioner or health visitor, and the child referred to a paediatrician. Following a full assessment by the paediatrician, a further referral to a specialist hospital consultant may be made. Paediatricians usually see the child and family regularly and are key members of the support team, ensuring that the child's health, medical and therapeutic needs are met. With the school doctor, they are the closest link with the medical network for the parents and school and the key person to advise the family and to discuss the prognosis and likely outcomes of medical procedures and operations. They liaise with other hospitals, doctors, consultants and therapists looking at the child's medical, physical and emotional needs. A child with severe motor difficulties may also have hidden problems with spatial awareness, perception, concentration, speech vision or hearing and may also have emotional problems. The paediatrician will refer to other specialists for further assessments if necessary.

Social workers

Social Services

Social workers help families and children with special needs to cope with disabilities and associated economic, emotional and social handicaps. They coordinate the services which are available, working in schools, day and residential centres, hospitals and private homes. The structure of Social Services varies around the country and may include disability teams catering for all ages or specific teams for children under eight or families and children. Social workers are mainly funded by local authorities and require professional training and a qualification in social work. The education social worker is employed by the LEA and used to concentrate on investigating absence from school, but their duties have now widened and may include investigating application for free school meals and duties such as financial help with school uniforms, exclusions and other general social work.

Chapter 3

School planning to meet the needs

The school philosophy

Positive attitudes of whole-school staff, children and their parents are crucial for successful inclusion of children with physical disabilities, and schools need to consult widely if they are thinking of developing provision for pupils with physical disabilities. The more people consulted, the more likely there will be a positive response leading to a successful philosophy and inclusion. Schools need to develop and be prepared to change, to learn and to take on new challenges if inclusion is to succeed. It is a process which takes time, commitment and hard work by many. LEAs and schools moving towards inclusion, need to plan with Health Services well in advance, to ensure that therapy and medical services are available as part of the support team for the school. Without long term planning, therapy and medical services may not be available and inclusion of children with severe motor difficulties is unlikely to meet the child's needs. Effective arrangements and working policies with other services are vital. So often lack of communication and planning between services hinders successful inclusion.

Admissions to schools

Schools need to look at their current admissions procedures, provision of specialist facilities and policy on inclusion, access and specialisms and should identify key areas which may need reviewing. The school SEN policy should have clear targets and criteria for the whole school, evaluated at the end of each year, with the information passed to the governing body. Schools need to ensure that children with SEN are not disadvantaged and that the school's mission statement is reflected in its SEN policy. The 6/94 Circular, (DfE 1994c), gives guidance on suitable admission arrangements (for those without a statement).

> While LEAs and school can make any reasonable and objective admissions arrangements in the event of oversubscription, those arrangements cannot be used to refuse admission to a child – or give the child lower priority than other applicants – simply because the school considers that it cannot cater for his or her special educational needs.

> The school's SEN policy should state whether the admission arrangements

> give priority to children with some SEN, and the criteria used ... where the school is accessible to pupils with disabilities, the SEN policy should also specify whether the school or LEA gives priority in admitting children who could make use of those facilities, including access arrangements. The number of places allocated under special criteria for educational reasons should not exceed 10% of the total intake.

> (DfE 1994c, paragraphs 34 and 35)

There is no doubt that accessibility is a key issue for pupils with severe motor difficulties. Some schools have been adapted, but the vast majority of ordinary mainstream schools do not have adequate, functional access.

School governing bodies have important duties towards pupils with SEN (DfE 1994a 2:6) and must do their best to see that the necessary provision is made for any pupil who has SEN. 'Whatever arrangements are made in a particular school, statutory duties remain with the governing body.' (DfE 1994a 2:8.)

School governors

Following possible adaptations to buildings, and planning, consultation and team-building with other services and the LEA, the school is ready to take pupils with physical disabilities. Staff need to be aware of the physical and medical needs of pupils, as well as their educational needs. It is tempting to see children with the same disability as having the same needs, but this is not the case. Though similar in many ways, children with the same condition are very different, requiring different treatment and handling. The most important point is that they are children first, and have the same needs as every other child. A multi-disciplinary meeting involving as many team members as possible will enable the school to establish an accurate, up-to-date picture of the needs of the whole child. It may not be possible for all professionals to attend, but they should be invited and asked to send copies of relevant reports, meet at another time or talk on the telephone if they cannot attend. The school should be invited to attend the preschool annual review, whenever possible and this is an ideal time to arrange an informal meeting with professionals and parents before or after the review.

Meeting the support team

The school should run through a normal school day, listing questions which need to be answered for school and parents. Transport to and from school is an important part of the school day, which needs some planning.

What is needed to meet the child's needs?

- How will the child get to school?
- If provision of transport is required, is it clearly written in the statement?
- Are there enough disability parking spaces in the car park or street for parents or taxis near an accessible entrance?
- Have other parents been consulted about disability parking spaces and do they agree in principle?
- Is there parking space for a bus near a school entrance?
- Are the transport escorts allowed to take the children into school or is the policy that they remain on the bus?
- Are escorts allowed to take the child from their own front door into the bus or are parents expected to do this?
- Are parents and school staff aware of the transport policy and guidelines?
- Are transport staff trained in the special requirements of the children, e.g. epilepsy, communication aids, the child's ability to move or transfer independently?
- Is there an emergency procedure for the bus driver if a child has a fit or needs medical help?
- Are appropriate seats, seat belts or restraints for wheelchairs available in the bus?
- Have recommendations from wheelchair makers been checked to ensure that the wheelchair is safe to travel in when clamped down?

- Is there an assistant to meet the child at school and does the assistant's contract cover time before and after school?
- If an assistant or the bus is unexpectedly late, who will take charge?
- Do escorts wear official badges or a uniform, so that they are easily identifiable if the escort or driver has to be changed at short notice?
- How will school and parents be contacted if transport is late arriving or leaving school and who will pass the messages on to the relevant staff/parents?
- Will the child be expected to line up with the rest of the school in the morning or will they need to use the toilet first?
- Are school staff, child and parents happy with transport arrangements, and if not, what can be done?

Questions to ask about mobility around school

The school day necessitates a lot of movement around the school which needs to be planned, minimising movement as much as possible. Teachers also need to be aware of the time required by any particular pupil to move.

- What equipment has been recommended by therapists for mobility around school, PE, games, music and movement, in the playground and on school trips?
- Who will fund the equipment, and will it be in place before the pupil starts school?
- If the pupil needs to use a buggy or pushchair in school has this been discussed with parents and pupil and talked over with peers? This may make a difference to how the pupil is perceived by peers.
- Who will contact parents if the child needs to use a buggy or pushchair for a school trip? Has this been discussed with the pupil if they normally use a walker, rollator or wheelchair?
- When will each piece of equipment be used and where will it be stored when not in use?
- Is use of each piece of equipment clearly written into the IEP? When and how it is to be used, for how long and what quality of movement does it allow?
- Has thought been given to how the pupil will carry their books, small equipment and possibly laptop computer around the school and who will monitor this?
- Has the timetable allowed for two people from the support team to lift or position a pupil in equipment, if necessary?
- Whose responsibility is it to regularly monitor and mend the equipment and who will fund this?
- If equipment unexpectedly breaks, is there a spare wheelchair or major buggy available in school with safety harness and have parents and therapists agreed on its use?
- If electric wheelchairs are charged in school overnight, is there a safe, well-ventilated area to use and who will be responsible?
- If a piece of equipment is allowed to go home for weekends or holidays have parents accepted responsibility for its insurance and has this been agreed by the provider?

- Where will the equipment be stored when it is no longer needed in school?
- What is the procedure for wet playtimes?
- Has every attempt been made to give the pupil independent access around the school?
- Are all ramps and steps safe in school and the playground?
- Are any out of bounds areas clearly identified and do staff know?
- Are lifts regularly checked? Who is responsible for monitoring and contacting the firm if they break down?

Equipment in class

Children with severe motor difficulties are likely to require specialist seating, other equipment and resources. Younger pupils should not be placed in the same position for more than approximately 45 minutes to an hour, depending on the child and the impairment. They may need to stand as part of their therapy to avoid contractures, stretch the muscles and weight-bear. Often a pupil is better able to access the curriculum in a particular position, allowing them optimum use of their fine motor skills and speech. Floor sitters enable the pupil to sit on the floor with the rest of the class. Many of the questions raised about equipment for mobility are also relevant to chairs, standers and other equipment.

Questions to ask about specialist equipment

- Who is responsible for moving specialist seating if it is required at lunch times or for another lesson?
- Has a risk assessment been carried out for adults expected to move equipment around the school and what is the school policy on this?
- Has the equipment been ordered with lockable wheels and have the adults shown how to move the chair safely to avoid damage to the chair and themselves?
- Does the manufacturer recommend that a chair can be moved with the pupil sitting on it or should it be moved without the pupil, for safety reasons?
- Does the pupil's wheelchair have a tray, which will place activities in a good position?
- Is an accessible locker available, particularly for secondary pupils, to store small pieces of equipment such as laptops?
- Have teachers and assistants been advised on classroom management with good lighting and best positioning for the pupil, to enable access to all their specialist equipment, to ensure they are able to hear and see the class teacher without turning their bodies, have access to an electric socket if required and easy access to an exit so they may leave the class with least disruption?

Questions to ask about therapy

It is good practice for school staff to have liaised with other services, had some training and be able to understand the therapist's role. It is important to establish the therapy requirements of each individual pupil.

- What therapy will be required in school and will this be provided by Health?
- Will the therapist be a locum on a short-term contract or a permanent member of the therapy team? This is quite crucial for ongoing teamwork.
- Do parents pay for any private therapy and if so, how will the therapist liaise with the school and support team?

- How much therapy is planned for the pupil and when will it be reviewed?
- Will therapy mainly be for monitoring or hands-on treatment?
- Will parents routinely be invited to therapy sessions or only on occasions?
- Is there a suitable room in school available for therapy every day, some days or part of a day?
- Will daily therapy be required to be carried out by the assistant, under the direction of the therapist and will liaison time for staff be built into the session?
- Are parents happy for school liaison to be part of their child's treatment session or do they and the school feel it should be in addition to treatment sessions?
- Have therapists considered liaison time in their timetable and planning?
- Is the therapist happy for other school staff to attend some therapy sessions on a regular basis, e.g. class teacher, SENCO or second key worker?
- Is the therapist happy to work in the classroom regularly or when appropriate, with liaison time set aside afterwards?
- Is the therapist occasionally available to meet with the whole support team?
- Will the therapists be able to attend annual reviews and will this replace a treatment session?
- Are therapists able to train staff in lifting and handling or is a specialist training course required?
- If the pupil requires swimming or hydrotherapy as part of therapy, who is responsible for organising and funding transport and an escort?
- Is an assistant required to go into the pool with the pupil and if so, is this clearly stated on the assistant's contract?
- Are there regular training sessions for staff and parents for signing, e.g. Makaton, use of symbols and high- and low-tech communication aids?
- Is there a therapist who specialises in specific areas, e.g. communication aids or access to computers and will the school have access to a particular therapist if required?

Assistant or super person!

Children with severe motor difficulties are likely to need assistance for their self-care, toileting, feeding, medical and physical needs, to enable access to the curriculum and to carry out therapy programmes in school. This is the role of the support assistant, described in Chapter 2. These assistants support pupils for their physical and often emotional needs and support the teachers in supporting their educational needs. Because inclusion of pupils with such severe difficulties is quite new for schools, there is no bank of trained assistants which schools can tap. Schools are dependent on placing an advert or recruiting from parents and adults in the locality. The majority of assistants will have had no training and yet theirs is a vital role in the successful inclusion of pupils with physical disabilities. The school should discuss the assistant's role with the support team and write a clear job description, so that the appropriate questions can be asked at the interview. Questions will vary dependent according to the school's and the pupil's needs.

Is the assistant prepared to:

- work as part of a support team?
- cover other jobs in school if requested, e.g. when pupil is absent?
- toilet pupils and change nappies, pads, deal with colostomy bags, etc?
- administer medicines, when required, under the direction and training of the medical team, including by tube and rectal diazepam?
- carry out physiotherapy, occupational therapy and speech and language therapy programmes, under the direction and training of therapists?
- work under the direction of the class teacher to enable pupils to access the curriculum?
- be trained in the use of technological aids such as computers or communication aids?
- lift and position pupils in and out of specialist equipment, under the direction of the therapists and with appropriate training?
- assist pupils with eating and drinking, including tube feeding?
- attend some training sessions after school if required?
- stay at school with a pupil in an emergency, e.g. when the bus is late?
- travel to hospital or home with a pupil in crisis in an ambulance or in a private car with a parent or teacher?
- work different hours if necessary e.g. start early, leave early?
- go into the pool with the pupil for swimming or hydrotherapy?
- accompany the pupil on school trips, both day and residential?

Types of questions to ask when interviewing assistants

Training of assistants requires better planning by LEAs and schools, with a pay structure and contracts reflecting the assistant's values and skills. Assistants in special schools are on a higher rate of pay, yet roles are very similar. Assistants in mainstream schools are likely to carry out daily physiotherapy, occupational therapy and speech therapy, under the therapist's direction, while in special schools, therapy is mainly carried out by trained therapists. For younger children, a trained nursery nurse (NNEB) may be considered.

It is important to establish the needs of the child through the multi-disciplinary team meeting. Most children with severe motor difficulties will have a statement and the wording is crucial. Statements of SEN should reflect all of the child's needs. Professionals involved should give the LEA comprehensive advice, so that statements can be worded clearly, avoiding ambiguity. Much of this section will depend on local LEA policies, ways of working and whether the child is in a mainstream, additionally resourced or special school in or out of borough.

It takes time to advertise and appoint any staff, so timing is important to ensure that the school is in a position to meet the child's needs. However, with the right philosophy and a degree of common sense and practicality, schools are often able to admit a pupil, having had a commitment to purchase specific individual pieces of equipment. It is very stressful for parents and pupils if children are kept out of school for want of a piece of equipment, which may not be vital in the short term. With a little imagination it is usually possible to find a way round

Wording and timing – when will the child start?

things and satisfy parents, school and the authority. It might be possible to borrow equipment on a temporary basis, although Social Services are often not happy for equipment, which they funded, to be used in schools, even on a temporary basis. A pupil may be able to use their wheelchair until a specialist chair arrives. The support team will advise the school on which pieces of equipment are essential and which are desirable. If the school, the parents and the therapists are happy with the intermediate arrangements, there should be no problem. In some cases the child will not be able to start school without specialist equipment or some form of mobility. In these cases the child might start on a part-time basis, depending on the pupil's mobility, parental wishes, whether transport can be arranged and whether a trained assistant is available. There is usually a way for the child to attend school for part of the day, until permanent assistance and equipment has arrived. Members of the support team will be able to advise to ensure safety. If any medical or emergency procedures or administration of medicines are needed, it is vital for them to be set up and staff trained by the medical team before the child starts school. Parents should always be involved and the school may set up a contract which both parties sign. The school may list what they feel they are reasonably able to provide.

Technology – computers and communication aids for new pupils

Some pupils may arrive with a computer or communication aid, having had an assessment, while others may have had no input in this area. The first multi-disciplinary meeting or annual review at a previous placement should give a clear idea of the pupil's fine motor and communication difficulties. The pupil may already be on a waiting list for an assessment, but if this is not the case, therapists need to advise school staff on how to meet the pupil's needs using low-tech aids. When parents, school and the support team feel that use of technology is required to meet the pupil's needs, an assessment should take place. Some occupational therapists and speech and language therapists are able to assess straightforward cases, but more complex cases will need to be referred to a specialist or a centre such as ACE or CENMAC (see Appendix 3 for addresses). Some schools may already have devolved funding, but others may need to approach the LEA for assessment funding. Any request for an assessment or equipment should be recorded at the annual review and added to the statement via the annual review report, if is it appropriate. Statement wording for any equipment should be clear and concise, with particular emphasis on who is responsible for providing the equipment, training and monitoring of its use. When the wording is agreed and the statement signed, it is the responsibility of the LEA to ensure that provision is made.

Awareness training for the whole staff

It is important for the whole staff, including school-meal-time supervisors, secretaries and caretakers, to have some knowledge of the pupil's difficulties and medical needs. Whole-school staff and peers will benefit from disability awareness training. Without this training, staff may expect pupils to do things which they cannot or should not do, but worse still, they may take over tasks which the pupil *can* do. Reception-aged children are capable of planning a home corner to include children in wheelchairs. Older pupils may be involved in planning the layout of the whole classroom to aid access and inclusion for a specific pupil. These children will grow up with a true awareness and understanding of disability. As with every other pupil, there may be cases of name calling, bullying and unpleasant behaviour, but these can happen in the best schools. The school behaviour policy should make sure such behaviour is always dealt with firmly. The most difficult time for children will probably be when they understand the reality of their disability and the fact that it will not go away and they may never play football or ballet dance. They will benefit from counselling or a designated person to whom they can talk privately.

The benefits of inclusion are enormous and, long term, will change society's view of disabilities in a positive way. These children are the employers and employees of tomorrow. Growing up together is a right which belongs to every child. However, for some children, special school may remain the right choice for some or all of their educational lives, but better links between mainstream and special schools can include all children in society for part of their lives. The main aim is to meet the needs of each pupil and it is up to the support team, Health and Education to be imaginative and flexible in how those needs are met.

Conclusion

Chapter 4

Organising timetables, equipment and procedures

Planning the timetable for pupils with severe motor difficulties is always a complex affair. These pupils require time for activities in addition to the curriculum. There is just not enough time to do everything and priorities need to be set. Mobility and continence may not have been established, the pupil may not have had a full diagnosis and may also have visual, spatial or perceptual difficulties or problems with hearing, vision or learning, not yet diagnosed. Some children with physical disabilities attend school when they are four years old, having spent half their lives in hospital and it is impossible to diagnose or predict all of their needs. Timetabling for individual needs must be flexible.

Teachers are trained to plan and deliver the curriculum, but may not have had training on disabilities. Physical and medical difficulties may arise, which have to be dealt with immediately, such as therapy following an operation or the start of epilepsy. The needs of the child will dictate the timetable and planning to a great extent. A child standing or walking for the first time will need regular daily therapy sessions, which although time-consuming, will increase their quality of life. Crisis periods could arise requiring delicate and sensitive handling for the child, parents and family. By secondary school the pupil's physical, medical, learning, social and emotional needs are better established, unless the condition is deteriorating or recently diagnosed. Pupils are more often able to communicate their own needs and their mobility level and toileting needs are well established.

Points which may help when timetabling

- Ensure there is one IEP covering all areas of the child's needs (therapies, educational, emotional and behavioural) with achievable targets, reviewed regularly.
- Keep up to date with physical, medical and home developments.
- Use available time well by introducing more than one element into curriculum tasks, to cover various curriculum and therapy targets together.
- Include therapy and life-skill targets throughout the day.
- Link visits to the toilet with out-of-class activities.
- Timetable toileting or therapy if two people are required to lift.
- Link mobility therapy to movement around the school.
- Include standing therapy in general class activities.
- Introduce basic speech and language therapy aims into the curriculum via curriculum games.
- Include strengthening fingers, arms and upper torso therapy in curriculum activities.
- Arrange joint therapy sessions for children with similar needs. Assistants may then share the responsibilities, allowing them time to prepare work or liaise.

- Make a small booklet for each child with curriculum questions specific to the individual to practise when doing stretches or long toilet sessions, e.g. counting, one more, one less, mental arithmetic, what did the Romans wear?
- Plan support and activities for inclement weather at break times for vulnerable pupils.
- Timetable swimming or other physical activities to replace lessons which may not be practical, such as rugby for a boy with Duchenne's muscular dystrophy.
- Try to match the curriculum timetable with the therapy timetable to ensure that the pupil has some quality time for both.
- Wherever possible therapy should not be timetabled during a subject lesson which occurs only once each week.
- If the pupil has to be withdrawn, try to make it at a different time each day.
- Ensure that senior managers are aware of the needs of pupils, so that when class changes are planned, the pupil has minimal movement around the school.

Equipment issues – schools and parents

Therapists working with the pupil will assess the pupil for equipment and it is important that these assessments are carried out in partnership with school and parents. It is little use requesting the LEA to fund a large, expensive stander if the school does not prioritise its use. If parents have been committed to a particular therapeutic philosophy such as conductive education, they may not want their child to be strapped into a supportive chair, unless there has been a great deal of discussion, planning and agreement beforehand. Sometimes compromises have to be made, especially if the pupil is moving schools or having difficulties accessing the curriculum. A well-written IEP, involving therapists and school and agreed by parents, will determine what equipment will be used, how and when.

Different positioning aids blood flow, promotes bone development, avoids long term damage to skin, is more comfortable and avoids muscle contractures, where muscles are locked in a certain position. We all know what it is like to attend a full day course sitting on the same hard chairs, although we are able to change our positions. The IEP needs to record seating, standing and positioning throughout the day. If the teacher is aware of the reasons for specific positioning, they will ensure it also happens in those flexible times, when the timetable may not be in operation, such as a concert rehearsal.

Equipment recorded in the IEP

The school day is made up of a series of different activities involving large numbers of children inside and outside school. A mainstream school is designed primarily for able-bodied pupils who have no problems with mobility and are able to move in the hall and playground spontaneously, but children with severe motor difficulties also need to be included in all these activities. It cannot happen spontaneously, as with their able-bodied peers, and it requires careful planning and organisation. They may need to use a special piece of equipment such as a walker or a tricycle, and positioning takes time. It is very important that the child with motor difficulties is part of the action and does not always arrive when it is all over! Special schools are specifically designed to meet the needs of pupils with severe motor difficulties and therapists are often based on site. However, the same principle applies and any use of equipment should be planned with the agreement and understanding of teachers, therapists and the parents. The IEP should state what, where and how the equipment will be used.

Seating and positioning

Good seating and positioning is important for all pupils, but is particularly vital for those with motor difficulties. The type of seating and positioning is dependent on the pupil's activity and therapeutic needs. They might sit in a specialist, supportive angled chair for one activity, stand for another and may sit on the floor or a small stool, unsupported, at some time in the day. Greater postural support is necessary during activities requiring detailed fine motor work such as craft and writing. Less support may be needed for less demanding physical tasks, such as storytimes. Wherever possible, seating should be as near to the same height as their peers for the majority of the time, to enable them to socialise and work in groups.

Equipment

Chairs

Specialist chairs range from simple adjustable-height chairs with no straps and pommels to complex, fully-adjustable, tilting chairs with straps, pommels, head- and foot-rests. A good sitting position is normally ninety-degree angles at the ankles, knees and bottom/back, but children with more complex needs may also benefit from being angled forward or backwards, depending on the activity. The aim is to achieve good sitting and hand function and to avoid positions which encourage involuntary movements and contractures. It is particularly important to position a child well for independent recording, activities using pen/cil and paper, feeding, and any communication aid and access via technology. Unlike their able-bodied peers, children with severe motor difficulties cannot sit independently without having to concentrate on sitting and balancing. They may require supportive seating to enable them to concentrate on the task, rather than on sitting. Pupils with involuntary movements may need to stabilise themselves or inhibit spasticity by holding grab rails. The use of a tray attached to the chair ensures that activities are positioned at the right height if there is no available table.

Floor sitters

These come in different shapes and sizes with additions including pommels and straps, allowing adequate support for sitting on the floor.

Independent sitting

This can be achieved at story, assembly, TV times or when the class is required to sit, listen or watch. The assistant may be required to sit behind the child on the floor or stool to give verbal prompts and to stop the child falling. Stools at the back of the group can be used by other children. Care must be taken not to overdo this activity and the time limit should be listed in the IEP as recommended by the therapist. Teachers often talk longer than they had anticipated!

Standers

These meet a wide range of needs from supportive, weight-bearing standers, enabling the child to stand at the sand, water tray, table or desk, to prone standers which can be angled in a variety of angles, introducing weight-bearing gradually. Weight can be borne across the body placing arms and hands forward in a good position to access activities. This may be the best position for some pupils to access different activities and may be the safest position for eating. Weight-bearing builds and stretches the muscles in the legs and trunk and increases blood flow around the body, helps prevent contractures, builds bone strength and density and encourages deeper breathing, which in turn aids clearer speech. These are all long-term benefits which may increase the child's independence and help carers. Good liaison, planning and a well-written IEP are crucial if a stander is to be successful and staff, pupil and parents need to agree on its use and position in class. Every school is different, but it takes only a little common sense to avoid dangers.

Walkers

Being able to walk just a few steps can raise self-esteem and increase blood flow to the whole body, strengthen and stretch muscles and help to avoid constipation problems, which often go with lack of movement. Therapists will assess and monitor walking for an individual, guiding the school on distance, length and quality. Sometimes therapists aim for a few quality steps, rather than distance, and this needs to be taken into account when planning the IEP. Wherever possible, walking should be functional and included into the timetable and school day. Careful timetabling can ensure that the pupil leaves the class early or late to avoid the rush or may take the register to the secretary to practise quality walking. For long distances it may be easier for the pupil to use their normal long-distance method of mobility to move to an equipment storage area, changing to a walking aid for the last short distance. This is particularly important for any whole-school activities to avoid tiredness and enables them to achieve best walking in front of peers. Adults can also facilitate walking.

Tricycles

These are often used for therapy and mobility in school, playground, dance and games lessons and may be the child's only independent form of distance mobility, allowing them experiences and concepts of speed and direction which they would otherwise miss. Some pupils with severe motor difficulties may also have perceptual, visual, spatial or concentration difficulties and/or have difficulties doing two things at once. Riding a tricycle in the playground practises all of these areas, although they need close monitoring. Attaching a lead or pole to the back of the tricycle helps to maintain the child's confidence, allowing shared control with the assistant. This can be removed when the pupil is safe in a busy environment.

Storage of equipment

This can be an issue when space is at a premium, especially in mainstream schools, which were not designed to take large pieces of equipment. Each pupil is likely to have a number of pieces of equipment which all require to be stored in convenient places. Good teamwork and liaison with all staff about the need for each piece of equipment will avoid unwelcome comments about size and storage problems in front of either the pupil or parents. The family home is very likely to have been taken over by equipment and parents are well aware of the issues. Schools need to make an audit of available space-making plans for storage of equipment and charging wheelchairs overnight, which for safety reasons should be carried out in a large, well-ventilated room, rather than in a small enclosed area. A suitable storage area should always be thought of whenever new equipment is ordered, as well as planning for its movement around school. Consideration of height and weight are important for assistants and carers. Therapists and manufacturers will advise if wheels can be attached to move equipment more safely.

Schools should consider health and safety for all school staff, especially the assistants working with the pupils. It is just as important to meet staff needs as it is to meet the child's needs, if inclusion is to be successful. Space may also be needed to position the child on or in the equipment. Dignity for the child is important and sometimes a curtain gives enough privacy. Flexibility, teamwork and commitment to successful inclusion go a long way towards solving many equipment problems.

Toileting

Toileting a pupil with severe motor difficulties can be time-consuming. They may use a wheelchair with many straps and may require the use of a hoist or two people to lift. Visits to the toilet are better planned regularly throughout the day to ensure that there is the necessary staff and equipment available. For pupils with such severe difficulties it is better to avoid waiting until the pupil asks, although there needs to be an action plan if the pupil does request the toilet. Some children with severe motor difficulties suffer from constipation which can be quite difficult to cope with. Frequent urine infections may also occur so that pupils need to be taken to the toilet more often and miss a lot of lesson time. This is an issue which should be discussed with parents and the Health team, as it also affects the pupil's ability to learn. Long-term toileting strategies will be planned by the Health team to allow the pupil as much independence as possible as an adult. Operations are often carried out when the child is in primary school and staff require proper training and close links with the medical team and parents. Lifting for the toilet is a particularly difficult lift, necessitating specific training for each individual.

Toileting may become a priority for the pupil at any time and it is important for all staff, especially teaching staff, to understand the reasons. Privacy must always be considered, but there may be times when an adult is with the pupil for long stretches and the teacher may want to utilise the time. With a little imagination this can be done, dependent on the pupil and the situation. Teachers might make a list of areas of the curriculum which the assistant can carry out in the bathroom such as :

- counting in English and other languages
- counting backwards, one more than, one less than
- mental arithmetic, fractions, percentages, addition, subtraction
- spelling, rhyming words, reciting poems, telling stories, making up stories
- giving the definition of a word, e.g. what does supercilious mean?
- questions about current class topics, e.g. how did the Vikings go to the toilet?

Health and hygiene

- Books kept in the toilet should not be used anywhere else.
- Assistants should wear disposable gloves and aprons and ensure that nappies and cotton wool are disposed of properly in special bins provided.
- Soiled clothes to be sent home should be put into a bag without holes. Many schools recycle old supermarket carrier bags which have holes allowing bodily fluids to escape.
- Schools often think that a shower is essential for young, incontinent pupils, but showering a child with severe motor difficulties is not easy and requires an adult to be in the shower with the child, unless there is a half shower door. Using a shower chair is more appropriate, but wipes and cotton wool are usually sufficient for cleansing.
- Individual pupils' towels will require laundering and should be clearly marked with the pupil's name.
- Some pupils may need a clean, though not sterile, environment, to carry out medical procedures. Staff require training on the basic rules of hygiene. There should be a foot pedal-bin, anti-bacterial soap and cleanser for surfaces and hands and the floor should be washed with a mop kept solely for that purpose.
- A lockable first-aid cabinet is necessary and some drugs may need to be kept in a lockable fridge.
- An adjustable height plinth for changing pads allows pupils to be more independent and protects the assistant's back.
- An emergency bell and flashing light alarm should be installed.
- Two-way radios or a whistle ensure that the assistant can summon help wherever they are.
- Pads, cotton wool and wipes should be disposed of in the proper way. Special bins are normally provided for such waste.

Chapter 5

Time management

Not enough time

Many teachers are concerned about the practicalities of working in a large support team to support one pupil, when they also have to meet their other pupil's needs. There is no avoiding the fact that it is a complex process, but teachers should understand the importance of multi-professional working. New skills, teaching approaches and differentiation techniques learnt through working within a multi-professional team, will be invaluable in supporting many other pupils with a variety of special needs. The IEP and therapy timetable should be well established, allowing the teacher to plan the curriculum, ensuring that all pupils are in class when delivering key teaching points. It is inevitable that there will be times when pupils may be unexpectedly withdrawn and these 'emergencies' cannot usually be helped. They may be caused by medical or equipment problems, other pupils' problems, visiting professionals or because the lift has broken down!

Good liaison is worth it!

Great difficulties occur if the support team does not liaise, there is no key worker and little or no communication in the school. The teacher and assistant are likely to feel isolated from the support team and unaware of the input and targets of different professionals. Without this knowledge the teacher is unable to include these targets into the routine of the day and differentiate the curriculum appropriately. Because of lack of knowledge, the pupil may be positioned badly, unable to see the board or hear the teacher without turning their whole bodies. They may be placed next to pupils with other special needs, including emotional behaviour and learning, 'so that the assistant can help more children'. Their specialist equipment and computer may be placed around a corner or at the back of the room, isolating them from their peers for much of the day. The class teacher may feel that this is best for the pupil, but with little or no experience and no support they may make wrong judgements.

Teachers may also delegate therapy programmes to the assistant, expecting them to be carried out 'when there is time'. Because of a lack of understanding of therapy needs, teachers may leave therapy programmes totally in the hands of the assistant. Good liaison between teachers, assistants, therapists and support teachers helps to avoid this scenario. It is especially important for a pupil who receives all three therapies. Large pieces of equipment such as standers or special chairs should only be introduced in consultation with the teacher, parents and the pupil, who all need to know how, when and why the equipment is necessary. Without adequate liaison the teacher, pupil or parents may not be happy with its use.

Am I on my own?

Teachers have been under a great deal of pressure following the recent government changes in education. They have to do more and more for a wider range of pupils, without further training. Teachers may be totally committed to the philosophy of inclusion, but it is easy to understand their concerns when asked to teach pupils with severe motor difficulties for the first time. However, as part of a large support team, the anxieties and concerns are shared and there are other professionals to advise. Time management is still likely to remain a key issue. How can teachers cope with professional input from so many people? There are a number of procedures which make good use of time, but it is up to the school, the support team and the teachers to decide what will work for them.

With so many people in the support team it is essential to have a keyworker and the most likely person is the SENCO, although it could be another member of the school-based team. The keyworker:

Keyworker

- liaises with all members of the support team and parents;
- ensures that teachers and assistants are kept up to date and trained when necessary;
- organises cover to allow teachers to attend a therapy session at the beginning and possibly halfway through the year;
- manages the support assistants; and
- plans for their regular attendance at therapy sessions.

It is also important for the keyworker to attend individual therapy sessions, possibly on a rolling programme and liaise with outside professionals face to face, through reports, telephone, individual programmes and liaison forms. The keyworker holds information from all support team members and it is their responsibility to make sure this information is recorded and passed on to other members of the team.

Quality liaison is the foundation for quality support. It is important that school staff understand and value the philosophy of working with all aspects of the whole child within the support team. It is important for staff to know who is in the support team, how they can be contacted and have clarification of their roles. Members of the support team also need to have updated records in a clearly presented format.

It is important that information recorded by the support team is quickly and easily found. The simplest way is for every member of the support team to use the same liaison form as a record of their input. Visiting professionals usually write up their own notes and, to avoid duplication, it is possible to agree to use the same liaison form (see Figure 5.1). Parents who live a long way from school may also be sent photocopies of liaison forms.

The liaison form for the A4 file

An A4-sized ring binder can be the basis of a liaison folder to store timetables, reports, programmes, IEP and up-to-date information to move around the school with the pupil. It should be easily recognisable and attractive to younger pupils, perhaps covered with holographic paper. A filofax-sized folder is more appropriate for older pupils. Establish where the folder should be kept in the classroom. The folder should include a map of the school, break times and an information sheet for visiting professionals, assistants and teachers who do not know the pupil or school well. The information sheet should show a run-down of the day including:

Individual support folder

ANY SCHOOL
LIAISON FORM FOR THE SEN SUPPORT TEAM

Name _____ Job Title _____

Date _____ Time _____ Class _____

Pupil Name _____

Reason for visit _____

Liaised with – SENCO – Class teacher – Assistant – Parent – EP – Other _____

INFORMATION

ACTION

To be copied to – Parent – SENCO – Class teacher – Physio – SLT – File – Other

Figure 5.1 Liaison form for the support team

- time, procedure and place for arrival and home time
- equipment required throughout the day and where it is stored, linked to the timetable
- procedures for break and lunch times
- reference to special care, therapy or medical procedures with named adults
- reference to procedures for administering medicines with named adults
- details of any emergency medical procedures with named adults
- fire procedures (these may differ in different areas of the school)

Dividers should be used to separate support team areas, e.g. physiotherapy, occupational therapy, speech and language therapy, hearing, vision, LEA and outside professionals, home links. Under each section file:

- the appropriate therapy timetable, dates of planned visits for each of the professionals and copies of individual therapy programmes
- copies of filled-in liaison forms recording a brief report of any visit, detailing any concerns and further action required

Remember:
- *This is an open file and should not include anything which cannot be shared.*
- *No assistant should carry out therapy or medical procedures without being trained by the appropriate professional.*

Individual liaison meetings with the keyworker continue to be vital, with only occasional whole support team meetings arranged around the pupil's annual review when many team members are likely to be available. There should be no big surprises for the annual review. Ongoing liaison means that problems can be addressed as they appear. The whole support team needs to be well aware of any issues, equipment or assessment requests before they are brought up at the annual review. This gives team members from the various services time to explore issues and consult their line managers, so that parents go home with answers rather than questions.

This is based on the same principle as the folder for younger pupils, but is a looseleaf folder the size of a passport or small filofax, including a small diary. Secondary-aged pupils often have a school diary which can be split at the centre fold and punched with holes. Additional sheets and dividers can be added and the whole thing put together in a small ring binder or with a spiral binding machine.

The passport will be individual to each pupil and may include:

- a passport picture of the pupil (optional)
- a brief list of how their disability affects them in the form of needs, such as regular medicine, time to move from class to class, understanding if homework is not completed on time
- guidelines of what to do and who to contact in an emergency
- agreement to leave certain classes early or to arrive late for others
- named friends (with passport photographs if appropriate) to carry laptops and bags, stay inside with the pupil when it is cold or wet, photocopy handouts, carry lunch trays, etc.
- small liaison sheets for therapists and visiting professionals
- times when the pupil can use the support base
- agreement to use specified computers or printers around the school
- agreement to use different pens, e.g. felt-tips instead of fountain pens, or to use laptop computer or word processor
- information about any specialist equipment needed such as table, chair, high stool or angle board
- communication aid information, detailing when and where it is charged and names of staff members trained in its use
- agreement to sit near an electric socket in class to use specialist equipment
- information about any hearing impairment, radio mikes or aids used
- information about any visual impairment, ideal size of print required and any specialist equipment, e.g. close-circuit television (CCTV)
- a description of the best seating position in various classrooms.

Most pupils can communicate with speech and are able to take responsibility for themselves, by passing on information to the different professionals. Pupils should inform adults if transfers are wrongly handled, if they feel unsafe and when it is time to use a different piece of equipment. This is a useful life-skill for any child who will always need some physical assistance.

The passport gives the pupil confidence, knowing that their needs will be understood, especially with new teachers or assistants. Every pupil and their passport should be discussed at a staff meeting to ensure that staff are aware of any emergency procedures or need for medication. It should be signed and agreed by pupil, parents and school.

When setting up the passport, it is important to involve and discuss the procedure with the pupil and the whole-school staff and to list all

The secondary school passport

support team members, making sure that everyone understands the process. It is important that each member of the support team is involved in the design and development of the passport and agrees on its use. It should then be the responsibility of each team member to communicate with the rest of the team using the passport.

Home/school liaison books

Home/school liaison books are invaluable for links with parents and home. They can be included in the folder by either punching holes in the book or using a slip-in plastic wallet. Sometimes books may be lost and if there are any misunderstandings between school and home it might hold important evidence. Blank liaison forms can be given to parents instead of using a book. They may be sent home for parents' use and placed in the office, where they can be easily reached by the various professionals. Carbon paper can be used successfully, but if the sheets are photocopied it is a good idea for them to be copied on the same day each week by an assistant or parent volunteer. Folders can be collected, liaison forms copied, filed appropriately and the folder returned to the pupil the same day. The SENCO should also keep a centrally stored copy.

Setting the goals — the IEP

Normally schools set short-, medium- and long-term goals for the whole school, planning the delivery of the curriculum with these goals in mind. This works well, ensuring continuity for each pupil, subject, year group and school as a whole. Pupils with special needs also have an IEP to ensure that there is proper planning in the curriculum and provision to develop the pupil specific areas of need. IEPs may be reviewed termly or more often and should be written with achievable targets to allow the pupil to progress at their own pace, ensuring success. Parents should be informed and consulted about the IEP, so that they can also support the aims and targets in the home and have a clear picture of their child's progress.

Long-term plan towards adult life-skills

Time is not on the side of the child with severe motor difficulties, so every moment is valuable from the day the disability is recognised. It is a good idea to devise a long-term, life-skill plan for children with severe motor difficulties and for families to work towards achievable short-term targets towards the long-term goals. Therapists and early years specialists need to explain their aims to parents from the outset, linking tiny steps to life-skills. On entering school it is important for the support team to revise and build on the plan. Class teachers can feel that the pupil has made little progress and not understand the length of time it takes for an individual to achieve certain skills. A teacher may only have the child for one year and it is impossible for them to formulate life-skill plans in the timescale available. Teachers must therefore be willing to work towards these very long-term plans, even though they may not see their hard work rewarded.

For example, the support team may believe that long term, a pupil might be able to use a computer to access the curriculum. Short-term strategies need to be formulated to move towards this goal. If the pupil has very little voluntary control they might push, knock, touch or hit a particular object, aiming towards grasp and release of the object, then prod and push playdough to strengthen and isolate the index finger.

Working towards these short-term targets will help the pupil achieve the long-term target of using a switch or keyboard to access the computer. Parents, teachers and assistants need to understand the reasoning behind these activities, which may appear far removed from the target! The long-term goal might take years to achieve and individual teachers will not see the final result. Understanding the reasons for activities will ensure teachers give them priority.

One of the difficulties in working collaboratively across services is the problem of the separate funding and management systems of Health, Education, Social Services and voluntary agencies. Successful teamwork between services needs agreement at local policy level, so that funding and provision can meet changing needs. Effective teamwork requires joint managing of joint provision from an LEA, working in a multidisciplinary and collaborative way and supporting schools and parents and children in the home. Problems faced by individuals can often be solved if their difficulties are seen as aspects of whole child, within a family.

A cross-service team

Difficulties can be caused if only one assistant is trained to meet the needs of an individual pupil, especially for toileting, feeding, positioning use of specialist equipment, handling and therapy programmes. The assistant's absence can cause a great deal of distress to the pupil, parents and school and places an intolerable burden on the assistant, who inevitably has feelings of guilt. This situation can be avoided by appointing a first and second keyworker assistant for each pupil, working as a team of supporters in the school. Both assistants should attend therapy sessions on a regular basis, perhaps alternating or together, and keep each other up to date through timetabled liaison and the support file. Linking two assistants in this way means that the second keyworker can move to be the first keyworker in the next class.

Assistants, job shares and first and second keyworkers

Changing the assistants yearly at a half term, rather than in September, ensures that there is an adult who knows the child and understands their need for seating, positioning, toileting, feeding, computer software, peripherals and access to the curriculum. It is better to avoid having a new teacher and a new assistant at the same time. This teamwork can be much more easily achieved in schools where there is more than one assistant allocated to individual children, but where there is only one pupil with severe motor difficulties in the school, try alternating with a school medical welfare assistant, nursery nurse or appoint two assistants as a job share. Pupils should not become overdependent on any one assistant, or the assistant overinvolved with the child.

At present less than half of LEAs provide appropriate assistant training. Most assistants are on low wages with short-term contracts. Considering that assistants are 'central to successful SEN practice in mainstream and special schools' (DfEE 1997) the situation now needs to be reviewed. Plans for training assistants are welcomed, but there is also a desperate need to look at contracts and wages. Short-term contracts give no security to assistants and give them very little incentive to accept long-

Assistant training and contracts

term training opportunities if, at the end of the day, they receive no more money and no more security. All of these issues need to be dealt with if we are to move towards further inclusion for pupils with SEN, especially those with complex physical and medical needs.

There are a number of recognised training qualifications for individual assistants offered locally and through universities and colleges. However, it is important that training is also carried out together with teachers, with a whole-school approach. Training assistants in isolation, away from their schools, can cause problems if the school is not involved or aware of course content and not able or willing to support the assistant. Teamwork involves ongoing training between professionals to ensure understanding of all the issues and to set up workable liaison procedures. Working together as a team is always better than working in isolation.

Part Two:

Practical ideas to access the curriculum

Chapter 6

Including therapies in the curriculum

This book highlights the importance of partnership between services and advocates that teachers or assistants should not take on the role of therapists, but work in partnership with them. Teachers will feel more confident as part of a support team and be able to include therapy programmes within the curriculum. No member of a school staff should alter or set up a therapy programme, without the therapist's involvement and, if at all unsure, schools should always check. Any specialist seating arrangements must never be altered; however, if staff feel that there is an element of danger, because equipment is unsafe, it is best to contact the therapist for advice and not to allow the pupil to use the equipment. Serial numbers and full details of all equipment should be kept in the pupil's file in case of damage, so that lost screws or new arms can easily be ordered.

The answer is both! It is clearly not possible for any speech and language, physiotherapist or occupational therapist, to achieve all therapy goals in one treatment session a week. Individual sessions with therapists remain vital for continual assessment and treatment, and for extending therapeutic goals. However, ongoing therapy within the curriculum and in daily living is possible through training parents and school staff although there are still likely to be physiotherapy stretches and other therapy targets best carried out at home or school in a quiet, private environment. The ultimate goal is for the young person to become as independent as possible and to participate in life-skills and activities in the best way they can.

One of the main difficulties for teachers is the time taken out of class to carry out therapy programmes, so that pupils miss out on important lessons. Much of this can be avoided if therapy is included as part of the curriculum or functional mobility around school, leaving out-of-class therapy sessions for specific, timed sessions. In close liaison with therapists, teachers are able to understand therapeutic aims and include them in educational tasks or games, within the curriculum. Teachers should ask themselves: 'How can I introduce speech and language therapy, physiotherapy, occupational therapy and other curriculum targets into this task?'

Continuous assessment and good record-keeping is the key to success. Therapists will provide a therapeutic baseline, doctors a medical baseline, while teachers need to establish a baseline for the pupil's cognitive abilities. This will produce a clear picture of what the pupil

Partnership with therapists is the key to success

Should therapy be at 2 o'clock on a Thursday or incorporated into daily living throughout the day?

How can therapy be included in the curriculum?

Record-keeping and establishing a baseline of skills

37

can achieve and should form the basis of the IEP. It will not be possible to include all targets in the IEP, but it is important to choose targets from each area on the statement. The next step is to record how the targets will be achieved in the curriculum as part of the IEP. Targets such as independent walking or sitting should be recorded on the timetable and IEP, with clear records and plans showing when, where and how they will be achieved such as:

'AIM – To sit independently on a stool 3 times weekly for 10-minute sessions with adult support for safety and to monitor and record. With success 6/6 times increase time by 1 minute'.

Common therapy targets to include in the curriculum

Although therapy targets are specific to individuals, there are many common targets which are appropriate to a great many pupils. The therapy programmes will clearly list aims and objectives and should, wherever possible, be included as part of the curriculum.

Using fists, together and separately – voluntary movement

Pupils who are only able to use fists should practise using two fists together, then left and right separately. With differentiation and imagination many games and activities can be devised, within the curriculum and daily living, to teach and practise voluntary control and directionality, as well as curriculum concepts using only fists. Games involving pulling or pushing objects with cards mounted on blocks, objects, counting, matching numerals, letters to words or words to objects, matching colours, use of table-top scissors and playing rhythms on a drum, can be achieved by using the fist.

Grasp, hold and release

Being able to pick up, hold (grasp) and let go of (release) objects is a crucial life-skill. Grasping comes before the ability to release, but if the pupil cannot release an object, the wrist, back of the hand or thumb should be gently stroked, which will cause the hand to open and the object to be released. Grasp and release activities can be included throughout the day at home and school in a lying, standing or sitting position. Any games involving picking up and dropping objects of different sizes, shapes and textures into various receptacles, or picking up and placing cards/blocks with letters, words or numbers onto a specific table-top area, will practise grasp and release. The pupil may need to start by using two hands together and, with success, practise left and right hands individually.

Bilateral – using two hands

Holding objects with two hands helps keep the head in midline enabling the movement of the head in all directions, without falling backwards or sideways, and helps balance for sitting and standing. By leaning forwards with both elbows stretched, in midline, looking at hands and objects, some children are better able to listen to instructions and concentrate. Larger objects such as balls can be lifted, pushed, pulled, moved or dropped. Cards should be mounted on long blocks which require two hands to lift, held on with velcro or two rubber bands. Long, thin boxes can be filled with different weights of sand to help build upper arm strength. Alternatively, a pupil with weak muscles can use cards attached to polystyrene or foam blocks.

Midline – keeping the body central

The midline is an imaginary line down the centre of the body. Being able to hold the head in midline enables the child to focus attention and concentration and helps develop eye/hand coordination. Holding something with both hands with stretched elbows gives fixation to the shoulder girdle, helping to bring the head into midline to aid balance. In class, the teacher should be positioned in front of the pupil, to avoid the body having to be turned, so reinforcing the midline position. There is a tendency for assisting adults to always sit on the same side of the pupil, forcing the pupil to use one side more than the other. Careful consideration should be given when placing items to make sure they are central to the pupil. The pupil should not need to stretch to either side and this will help balance and concentration on the task.

Some pupils have difficulties crossing the midline, but it is a necessary skill for writing and drawing. Crossing the midline may be both a physiotherapy and occupational therapy goal, depending whether it involves a fine or gross motor activity. Activities to cross the midline might include drawing or painting across a large area, reaching for, or placing, objects across the body or throwing beanbags across the body. Gross motor activities to cross the midline also help with fine motor activities.

Fixation and involuntary movements

Some children with cerebral palsy are unable to fix themselves in a position for controlled movement. Whenever they move one part of their body, another part will also move. When they speak often their legs will lift off the ground and when one arm is moved the other arm will also move and/or their head will move towards the opposite side. Many children also experience exaggerated reactions with the effort of movement. These are all involuntary movements and make life very difficult for the individual. It helps if children learn to fix themselves, instead of always being strapped into equipment. Some children may be able to sit unaided, but will need to concentrate very hard. In such circumstances it is unfair to expect them to also concentrate on the teacher or the curriculum. It is important to prioritise tasks and decide how best they can be achieved. Pupils may be well-supported in a chair, stander or on the floor for activities when they have to concentrate on key curriculum areas such as reading or fine motor control, but be expected to sit independently for activities such as listening to a story or sitting in assembly.

Startle reaction

Sudden stimulation or noise may cause startle reactions with the pupil showing exaggerated motor patterns. Those involved need to understand the need to approach the child quietly, allowing them to react positively and giving them time to calm down and respond. If a pupil has a significant startle reaction and is in a noisy environment, it is only fair to remove the pupil for short sessions to a quiet area for respite, and to consolidate and teach key curriculum and therapeutic targets. This should be included in the pupil's IEP with regular evaluation and good record-keeping. As pupils become more used to the environment, it is likely that the startle reaction will become less exaggerated, although it is unlikely to disappear.

Use of the open, flat hand

Pupils who can use an open, flat hand as well as a fist are likely to have greater independence. The aim is to use hands together then separately, grasping objects with elbows bent and straight, then lifting one hand off the table while leaving the other on the table. Pupils may need to fix themselves into position by holding on with one hand or anchor an elbow in order to use the other hand, which should also help their sitting position. Some children may need a light arm-splint for very weak wrists and to aid extension of the wrist to grasp and hold. Activities to encourage an open hand include making handprints, clapping, banging tambourines and drums, rolling playdough or plasticine, playing with hand puppets, washing hands, and any activity involving picking up and using a wide variety of different-sized objects, shapes and textures to sort and classify.

Isolating the index finger for fine manipulation

The index finger is used to point accurately to small items and for many other daily activities. It is valuable for communicating aids and keyboard skills enabling greater control with small icons and letters. This skill is a worthwhile target which may take a long time and lots of practice to achieve. Activities should be introduced which involve poking, pushing and pulling, dials, toy pianos, light and bell switches, finger puppets, resisting springs, tracing in wet sand, finger painting, pushing magnets on magnet boards, keyboards, switches, use of concept keyboards, touch screens. There are also many useful finger rhymes, songs and games.

Strengthening the index finger

Sometimes the pupil can isolate the index finger, but has very little strength to use it. Activities to strengthen fingers might involve rolling, squeezing, pounding, making holes and pinching playdough, plasticine or clay, pressing seeds into the soil, squashing bubblewrap, pressing switches and buttons on books and toys, using an old typewriter, finger puppets, using water pistols and squeezy water-spray bottles.

Pincer grasp – thumb and index finger together

The pincer grasp is one which is used frequently throughout the day and is made by the index finger and thumb touching or squeezing together. It enables fine motor control to pick up small objects and is used when holding a pen/cil, paintbrush, fork or other utensil in a tripod grasp. There are many activities to practise this movement including picking up and sorting small objects, flicking, squeezing, inset puzzles, magnetic boards, writing, drawing, painting, switches, keyboard, turning the pages of a book, finger puppets and actions to rhymes. The pupil should practise these in the air, on and off a table-top, when sitting and standing, with elbows stretched and bent.

Eye/hand coordination – visual motor ability

This is the ability to coordinate the eyes and body muscles to work together for a motor action, such as reaching for an object or writing. Various activities should be encouraged daily, lying, sitting and standing, and success with two hands should progress to use of either hand. Establishment of the dominant hand is important and will only occur if the pupil can choose which hand to use. If the dominant hand is not established, it can lead to poor interaction of left and right sides causing directional and laterality confusion. Activities involving reaching in different directions, positioning objects in, on or by other objects, pouring water or sand into various containers, marking, drawing or writing, rolling, catching, hitting, throwing balls into various-sized boxes or hoops, hitting suspended balls or balloons of various sizes all practise eye/hand coordination. Writing, copying and drawing require very good eye/hand coordination abilities.

Perception

This is the way the body interprets and makes sense of information gained through the senses. It involves making sense of shape, colour, size and the relationship objects have to each other and to the individual. 'It can be described in lay terms as common sense, understanding, 'nous' ... It also includes more complex abilities such as form constancy, appreciating an object from whatever angle it is viewed, and figure background discrimination' (Penso 1993: 3). Perceptual skills may be broken down into different areas and occupational therapists have specific responsibility to test and remediate perceptual problems.

Activities to help perception include matching activities using objects, photographs and pictures, puzzles and inset boards, sorting activities, matching sizes, pictures with differences and similarities, Kim's game, game of pairs, copying designs made with magnetic blocks, beads or objects, sequencing games to carry on or copy, using a torch or pointing to shapes and objects in the environment, using a finger puppet, feeling games, I-spy' or finding what is missing on a given picture.

Proprioception

This informs us about the position of our body in space. Awareness of posture and balance is gained from receptors in muscles, tendons and joints, eyes, vestibular apparatus in the inner ear for balance and the equilibrium of the body. Proprioceptive feedback helps us to remember the feel of movement or a change in body position. A child with difficulties in this area will have poor body awareness leading to difficulties with laterality and handedness, dressing, copying, drawing and may have reversal problems when reading and writing. The child should know their own body parts and understand and use the associated vocabulary.

Visual perception

This is the ability to understand visual information and make sense of what is seen. A visual-perceptual disorder may result in an inability to recognise objects, pictures, letters, numbers or words accurately, leading to poor performance with reading, writing, maths, drawing, recognising forms, shapes and sizes, cutting, sticking and copying.

'It has become increasingly accepted that difficulties in visual perception and problems in coordination and movement can all affect classroom learning. It is accepted that the two defects are associated' (Tingle 1990: 67).

It is important to consider the child's ability to pick out an object from a busy, detailed background (figure background discrimination) when choosing reading books. Print and pictures should be clear and uncluttered and books should be avoided which have too many words on a page, words on top of pictures or dotted about the page. Differentiate by covering half the page with a piece of plain card or enlarging and cutting the worksheet in half. Colour coding may help the pupil to find the right words or sentences. Refractive errors, such as long- and short-sight and astigmatism can be corrected with glasses, but there is no such aid for pupils who have difficulties with figure background. It is the teacher's job to ensure that work is appropriately differentiated. Pupils with visual perceptual difficulties should not be expected to copy from the blackboard. It is difficult for them to remember and transfer visually the work from a vertical surface to a horizontal one, especially if they are not sitting centrally to the board. This is also true for pupils with oculo-motor difficulties who have problems accommodating vision from a distance.

Auditory perception

This is the ability to register and make sense of what is heard. Tests of auditory perception include attention span, discrimination of sounds and auditory sequential memory, which is the ability to remember what has been heard in the right order. Activities which help the pupil to concentrate and focus on selective sounds need to be practised. The ability to listen to and understand what is being said is important for learning complex motor skills. Activities to help include copying rhythms, following simple instructions, matching and recognising sounds, playing two or three sounds or words one after the other for the pupil to remember, filling in the missing words or lines to songs and rhymes and practising word families and phonics.

Perceptual-motor difficulties

These involve much more than just motor difficulties. Motor activity requires motor planning (praxis) preceded by perception. Without these, behaviour appears 'clumsy' or uncoordinated. Sensory information is provided by the sense organs in the body and sensory information about the position of the body is provided by proprioception. Normal deficits of hearing and sight are usually easily diagnosed, but other deficits, such as diminished tactile sensation, imperfect visual convergence or poor proprioceptive abilities, are much harder to diagnose. To be effective, the motor planning element of a movement must be accomplished without conscious effort. Learning to drive is a good example to explain the need for motor planning. With time, the body learns the motor patterns required to change gear and conscious plans for every movement do not need to be made. A pupil who has motor planning difficulties must consciously plan their movements throughout the day.

Perceptual-motor difficulties may not be diagnosed until the child enters the education system when precise and complex, gross and fine motor skills and motor planning are required for many activities. In the home, eating, drinking and use of cutlery can be difficult for children with perceptual-motor difficulties. The child must know exactly where the mouth is in order to transfer food on a spoon or fork without visual monitoring. A conscious effort is required to transfer food to the mouth and if the child is startled or loses concentration, the head may be turned away when the spoon reaches the mouth.

Activities should be given which practise body awareness, such as 'Simon says' involving different body parts, games and songs involving left and right, copying actions, drawing round pupils, filling in missing eyes and other body parts, signs and actions in songs and rhymes, moving between large objects, walking in and out of hoops, tyres, boxes, rolling along the floor to reach a specific spot, following a simple map to find some 'treasure'.

Sensory defensiveness

Some children react negatively to some or all sensory stimulation or have difficulties processing sensory information. They may dislike noise (auditory defensiveness), light and direct gaze (visual defensiveness), tastes and different textures and stimuli near the mouth (oral defensiveness). This may limit their ability to function and the pupil will require a full assessment carried out by an occupational therapist, with a treatment programme devised and advice given to school and parents.

The sense of touch is very important to the development of the nervous system and affects learning, perception and daily living. A pupil who has tactile defensiveness may be advised to use a variety of mediums such as playdough, thick finger paint, glues and a variety of textures. A plastic container can be filled, for example, with lentils and curriculum objects hidden in the jar or the pupil may delve into the jar to find a specific object beginning with a letter, or a topic category such as farm animal. Other activities include texture snap, matching texture cards, walking on a variety of textures, texture books and concept keyboard texture games. The speech therapist will be able to help with oral defensiveness which is more likely to be dealt with in the home, although support and advice may also be needed in school.

Mobility

Grasp helps mobility by enabling the body to be pulled up from lying to sitting, sitting to standing or for walking around holding onto furniture. The pupil should be able to hold with one hand and release their grasp with the other. The ability to release grasp in both hands helps with sitting, standing and balancing and should be practised functionally, in everyday situations as well as in treatment sessions. A variety of types of mobility should be available throughout the day. Matching type of mobility to the timetable will ensure that pupils are not too exhausted for lessons.

Weight-bearing on flat hands

Pupils have greater independence if they are able to weight-bear on flat hands. Arms need strengthening to bear the weight of the body in crawling, kneeling and sitting. This helps the pupil to rise from sitting to standing using flat hands to push up. It also builds upper arm strength, which aids wheelchair mobility, transference and independence. Activities can be included in PE and movement lessons as well as daily routines. There are many leisure activities and sports which build upper arm strength including swimming, canoeing, archery, horse riding, tennis, basketball and other ball games which use the upper torso. Activities such as tug-of-war in sitting or standing position, pulling the body along a bench by the arms, swinging by the arms, pushing and pulling and lifting, and throwing balls and beanbags of increasingly heavier weights, also help.

Chapter 7

Practical ideas to introduce therapy into activities

Wherever possible specific areas of the curriculum and therapy targets should be covered in one activity, although care must be taken to ensure the activity is achievable both cognitively and physically. Simple games can be devised for younger pupils to learn basic colours, shapes, sizes, numbers, letters, words, etc. which will useful for the whole class. Games and activities can also be linked to curriculum topics such as the Romans or living things. The important element is to think laterally and devise *how* the activity or game will be played, including placement of items, size of objects, adaptations of cards, containers or templates used and utensils to be introduced.

Introducing objects or balls into a game enables occupational therapy targets to be practised, such as grasp and release, use of a flat hand, isolating and strengthening the index finger, pincer grasp, hand/eye coordination, bilateral activities, crossing midline, perception, body awareness, sensory/tactile defensiveness and others. Use of objects also gives the opportunity to introduce speech and language targets by introducing turn-taking, giving and following directions, use of particular initial or end sounds and consonant or vowel blends, directional words such as up, down, high, low and prepositions such as in, on, under, and many others. Occupational and speech and language targets should be used functionally in activities and included in everyday learning. For pupils with motor difficulties this meets their individual therapeutic needs, at the same time as meeting their educational, social and cognitive needs.

There are many different types of tongs, tweezers and squeezers and use of them helps to strengthen and isolate the index finger and thumb, increase finger dexterity and fine manipulation, develop hand/eye coordination and replicate regular scissors and spring-loaded scissors. Most games can be adapted to use tongs and tweezers by introducing objects or by attaching cards to blocks of foam, wood or polystyrene for ease of grasp:

- Tweezers may be squeezed to replicate a scissor action.
- Teabag squeezers have a light, simple squeezing action replicating the action of spring-loaded scissors.
- Salad tongs have a squeezing or scissor action and their size means that they may be used with both hands (bilaterally).
- Barbecue tongs are heavy with a squeezing or scissor action and are best used with both hands (bilaterally).

Use of spring-loaded clothes pegs encourages finger manipulation and dexterity, helping the pupil to become proficient in fine movements

Curriculum targets

Use of objects and balls

Tongs, tweezers and squeezers

Spring-loaded clothes pegs and clips

such as self-help skills, fastening buttons, holding pen/cils, isolating and strengthening the index finger and thumb and strengthening muscles in the wrist, hand and fingers. The action of squeezing a spring-loaded peg also replicates the muscles used for cutting with scissors. Pegs can be used for colour matching, counting, recognising body parts by pegging onto a doll or person, reading and matching words or letters to cards or objects by attaching pegs to the game cards.

Different pegs have different tightness of springs. Start a collection of pegs and clips of various strengths. Two pupils may use different strengths of spring to play the same game.

- Hair clips have the lightest scissor-type, spring action and are the easiest to use.
- Bulldog and paper clips have a wide variety of spring strengths.
- Clothes pegs are very cheap and come in different colours and sizes.
- Clamps used in wood and metal work have the same spring action as pegs, but have a very strong spring action.

Spoons

Activities involving spoons help feeding and self-help skills, encourage and develop fine motor control, hand/eye coordination and dexterity. The occupational therapist should always be involved in assessing pupils when introducing the use of tools, as there may be neurological reasons for using one tool rather than another. Care must be taken to match the spoon to the pupil and to think carefully about the box or bowl. Containers with straight sides are easier to use than those with rounded sides. Spoons have different depths, affecting the ease of use. Use spoons in sand or water play: 'Put the biggest/heaviest piece of playdough in the square box' or 'three spoons of sand into the orange bucket'. Pupils might read words, numerals, symbols or pictures on a card or be directed using speech, signs or symbols. Introduction of a barrier introduces turn-taking and giving directions.

It is important to establish the pupil's capabilities with a spoon and to start by using the spoon they would normally use, which may have an adapted handle. Spoons can be given grips in the same way as pencils and paintbrushes. Specialist spoons and hand grips are available.

- Teaspoons are probably the most useful spoons to start with, as they are used for self-feeding.
- Dessert-sized spoons can be held in one or two hands to pick up quite large objects.
- Cooking spoons (wooden, metal and plastic) are used in the kitchen and these might be used with both hands together, for example, picking up a beanbag or ball in PE. The game might cross the midline and build upper arm strength.

Tubes and guttering

These can be included in an activity to encourage and develop fine motor control, dexterity, grasp and release, hand/eye coordination and many other therapy targets. There are a whole variety of tubes of different widths and pliability, bought in DIY shops and used to make games where balls, marbles or objects are rolled down the tube into a container. Directions might be verbal, read from a card, symbols, signs or pictures. Games can be for one or two players, where one player rolls the object down the tube and the other directs the tube to the right area.

Objects and containers should be different sizes, colours and shapes and linked to the curriculum.

Tumble drier extractor tube

This is a very versatile tube which pulls out to about 5 feet long and can be returned to its original size of about 30 cms and stored in an A4-sized plastic wallet. Fun games can be devised and played by all pupils at any level. It can be used with a variety of balls to play skittles or a target game in PE. Speech therapy games can also be introduced by using the tube to amplify the voice.

Pliable tubes

Tubes wide enough to take balls, marbles or objects can be bought from chemist or DIY shops. Objects can be picked up by hand or with a spoon or tongs and dropped down one end. The other end is positioned so that the object falls into containers of different shapes and colours. Reading and maths games can be adapted where a card gives directions to 'drop three blue marbles into the yellow box' or '3+1 marbles in the blue basket'.

Ordinary cards can be adapted to make them easier to pick up. Care must be taken to ensure that any picture or writing is clearly printed and is of the right size, printed on the background to meet the needs of any individual pupil.

Adapting flash and games cards to be picked up more easily

Cards on foam

Many pupils with cerebral palsy and other impairments find it easier to pick up light, squashy objects, often using their index finger and thumb. Foam comes in sheets of different thicknesses and can be cut easily and exactly. Cards may be attached to the foam very simply, using one or two rubber bands. Alternatively, a piece of laminated card can be stuck to one side and ordinary cards fixed to the laminate with self-adhesive Velcro, Blu-tak or strong magnetic tape.

Cards on polystyrene

Polystyrene is very light and can be bought by the sheet in DIY shops.

Cards on wooden blocks

Cards can be attached to wooden blocks or toy bricks, using velcro, blu-tak or magnetic tape to be pushed or lifted.

Cards on carefully weighted boxes

Small plastic or cardboard boxes can be filled with sand or beans with different weights to increase upper arm strength. Longer boxes can be used for bilateral activities.

Self-adhesive magnetic tape

Comes in different widths and strengths and is easily cut. A small square stuck to the corner of a card enables it to be picked up with a magnet on a handle or sewn into the face of a finger or hand puppet.

Paperclips and magnets

Paperclips can be attached to cards, material, pages of a book or other objects and picked up with a strong magnet.

Simple equipment for adaptation

Velcro-looped material which sticks together

Velcro can be sewn or stuck onto clothes, shoes, cards and is bought by the metre in various widths. It is useful for anchoring toys, computer switches and equipment to the table-top or attaching cards and objects to display boards. Velcro is excellent for adapting clothes, and can be used instead of buttons on school shirt cuffs, ties, coat fastenings, clothes, shoes and trainers to aid independence in dressing and undressing.

Material which sticks to Velcro

This can be bought by the metre in different colours to make target games, speech therapy tabards and mats to anchor objects, toys, computer switches, etc. using Velcro fixed to the objects.

Knobs

Small knobs or beads can be attached to cards, puzzles and games by using a split pin or strong glue. Old beaded car seats are a good source of beads.

Throwing a dice

This can be difficult for pupils with motor difficulties. There are many dice of all shapes and sizes from specialist catalogues. Alternatively a dice may be enclosed in a large plastic, see-through pot with a lid and shaken with one or two hands.

Specialist pointers

These can be spun round to point to a number, letter or colour. They can be pushed or activated by a switch.

Boxes, tins, baskets, hoops and templates

A selection of different-shaped containers in different colours and materials introduces new learning elements and language into games. Templates may be used instead of containers, allowing complex, mathematical shapes to be used. Use of containers and templates also introduces directional and mathematical language, prepositions, hand-/-eye coordination, grasp and release, crossing the midline, pincer grasp, tactile stimulation and laterality. This depends on choice and placement of containers, objects used and how the pupil is given instructions. Velcro on the base anchors containers and templates.

Choose objects linked to the curriculum. Parents and children are often happy to help build a collection and charity shops and jumble sales are a good source. They could include:

- good quality plastic farm, zoo and wild animals
- real and toy household objects
- dolls' house furniture
- natural objects, such as pebbles, sticks, conkers, acorns and dried leaves
- plastic fruit and play food
- food packets and washed, safe cans and containers
- cubes and bricks of different colours, shapes and sizes
- dolls' clothes and real clothes
- artefacts linked to history
- play and real money, chequebooks, stamps, envelopes
- balls of different sizes, colours and textures, with sounds
- photographs or pictures of objects which are difficult to find, blocks, sorted and matched

and many more.

Store the objects by topic or in categories, such as animals, people, natural objects, using ice cream cartons, shoe boxes or zipper wallets for ease of use. Items required for a particular game should be kept in one zipper wallet. These same objects can be the basis for a variety of games at different levels.

Objects for games

An example of a curriculum game including therapy targets

A zipper wallet might include:
- objects – van, crocodile, zebra, tree, bicycle, man, hen, pig
- containers – red, square box and round, silver tin
- utensils – tongs, tweezers and squeezers added as appropriate
- container picture cards – red, square box and round, silver tin
- numeral cards – appropriate to the pupil, e.g. 1 to 8
- lower-case letter cards – initial sounds of enclosed objects
- word cards naming words of enclosed objects
- sentence cards, e.g. Put the hen in the red box using objects
- picture cards or photographs of enclosed objects
- body-part cards, e.g. fingers, fist, elbow, nose
- preposition cards in words, symbols or pictures, e.g. in, on, under
- record sheets to record different games:

   1. Cards with the lower case letters v, c, z, t, b, m, h, p. Match letters to objects or objects to letters.
   2. Cards with words. Match card to object or object to card.
   3. Cards with directions using pictures or symbols and one word, e.g. **hen in** (picture or symbol) **red box** (picture of red box).

Tongs, magnets or tweezers may be used.

4. Cards using two words – **hen in red box** (picture of red box).

5. Cards using three/four words – **hen in red box**.

6. Numeral cards and picture cards to show red, silver, circle or square. Pupil turns over the cards and places that number of items in the appropriate box.

7. Sorting games linked to the curriculum, such as: 'Put all the things that live/do not live in the square box', 'Put all the things with 4/2 legs in the metal box'.

8. More advanced reading games using cards can be made. These might involve erecting a barrier with the pupil directed by another pupil, e.g. 'Put the animal related to the alligator in between the two means of transport'.

9. 'What am I?' cards to read (linked to the objects) and the object placed in a container using tweezers, e.g. 'You can cross over me, I have four legs, I look like a horse, what am I?'

Many games to cover curriculum and therapy aims can be made using different objects and containers. It is a good idea to make a list of the objects, cards and containers and stick it to the zipper wallet. Clearly label cards and the wallet to ensure they are easily replaced.

Chapter 8

Computers and technology

Computers and technology have made a significant difference to people with severe motor and speech difficulties and are constantly developing. Computers can help pupils with disabilities to access the National Curriculum enabling them to record their work, do research work using CD-ROMs and the Internet and also control their environment, allowing them a greater degree of independence. The National Grid for Learning expects that by the year 2002 teachers will be confident and competent to teach using Information Communication Technology (ICT) in the curriculum and that there will be equality of access to take into account the particular, individual needs of learners. This has enormous training implications for all schools, if they are to meet the complex needs of some pupils. Mainstream schools need training in the use of a wide variety of specialist software and peripherals, and the importance of correct seating and positioning. Special schools also need training to cater for their more complex pupils and use of the computer as a communication aid. Therapists need on-going training for new developments in computer hardware, and peripherals, communication aids and adjustable-height furniture. *There must be a commitment to all pupils and all teachers, if there is to be true equality.*

The pupil's need for technology should be detailed in Section 3 of the statement of SEN and it is important that the wording is clear and unambiguous. Therapists and teachers need to advise the LEA on the pupil's need for appropriate technology. A full assessment should list hardware, software and peripherals required by the individual. The occupational therapist should be involved in assessments for technology and the positioning needed for access. Many parents ask for technology for home use, but LEAs usually provide equipment only for school use. A number of national and local charities purchase equipment for individuals in the home and if a communication aid is required, it should be jointly funded by Education, Health and Social Services.

What technology?

- An assessment will establish whether a computer is really necessary or whether a good, lightweight word processor meets the need for functional recording.
- Computer assessment centres such as Northern and Oxford ACE Centres and CENMAC will assess individuals (see Appendix 8 for addresses). The assessment should involve a team of professionals to ensure that all needs are assessed and met. The centres keep up to date with new developments, develop software and give advice and training sessions. Following an individual's assessment, equipment and software is recommended. They may lend equipment, but do not usually sell or arrange funding themselves.
- A computer will be necessary if specialist access peripherals are required and/or specialist software is needed for particular

curriculum areas and for predictive software and onscreen grids, to cut down the number of key strokes.

- If the pupil is unable to access the curriculum with pen/cil and paper, introduction to technology is important as early as possible. Pen/cil skills still need to be extended and developed, but the pupil may require technology as their main means of recording.
- It is important to ensure that pupils are not made to 'write' and their cognitive development held back, because of their physical difficulties with recording.
- Buy a computer with the highest specification and largest memory you can afford and ask advice from specialist computer centres such as ACE and CENMAC.
- Make sure the computer has the right specification to run specific software and a CD-ROM drive.
- A sound card and video card give aural feedback and are used in multimedia software.
- Headphones via a splitter will enable two people to listen to the computer without disturbing others.
- A modem is needed to use the Internet or Web pages.
- Consider the make of the majority of computers in the school. Schools normally have site licences for specific software to be used by the majority of pupils. Computer and software must be compatible.
- Consider the use of switches, rollerballs, concept keyboards, IntelliKeys and joysticks, and ensure that the computer has the right ports.
- Consider whether a desktop or laptop computer is more appropriate. Pupils with visual spatial or perceptual difficulties might have difficulties using a laptop successfully, although portable screens are now much bigger and thin film transitor (TFT) screens are much clearer and can be seen from different angles.
- Consider the computer's weight, and the need for transport between home and school.
- Consider the pupil's age. Laptops do not like being dropped, having things placed on top of them or playing in sand or water!
- Consider the length of time the computer can run on one battery charge. When and where will it be recharged? Is there an electric socket nearby in case it is needed?
- Some LEAs have an SEN computer specialist working within the authority who is able to advise and assess pupils with complex needs.

What am I able to do?

There may be difficulties in finding the right person to advise or carry out an assessment, or a pupil may be on a long waiting list at a specialist centre. What can be done in the meantime? Discuss with members of the support team and telephone an assessment centre for advice and ideas of what is needed. Involve the occupational therapist to ensure correct seating and positioning and a speech or language therapist may be able to advise on hardware, software, switches and other peripherals. The following points will need to be considered

Seating and positioning

This is important to ensure that the therapeutic, visual and medical needs of the child are considered. Some pupils may already have specialist seating in class and this may be the most appropriate and supportive seating for using the computer. It may not be feasible to purchase another specialist chair for the computer, so it is very important to ensure that the table, computer, screen, keyboard and switches are at the right height and angle for optimum functional use. In some cases a tray attached to the chair offers the best position for keyboards or peripherals. Alternatively the pupil might stand to access the computer, requiring the computer to be raised. Seating and positioning at the computer is the key to success and should always involve appropriate therapists, teachers and parents.

The table or computer trolley

An adjustable-height table or trolley is ideal for computers and can be positioned easily and accurately at various heights. It is a good use of resources, growing with the pupil to meet changing needs. A shelf is not required, but it is essential to have electric sockets which can be switched off. The pupil should not have to look up to the screen and down to the keyboard. The screen should be in the line of sight of the pupil's normal sitting position. Place the screen on the table with the keyboard in front and place the computer at the side with the printer on top. Schools often put the screen on a computer shelf and the keyboard underneath, requiring exaggerated movements looking up and down, which is not good for anyone.

Position of the computer in class

This should be considered to ensure that the pupil can see the blackboard, the teacher and other pupils in the class, if they are expected to work at the computer for any length of time. Another pupil might require less stimulation, away from peers, or out of class, in order to concentrate. This would be part of an IEP, evaluated and reviewed regularly.

Lighting

This should be considered to ensure that there are no reflections on the screen. Most computer shops sell anti-glare screens which can be attached.

Wrist supports

These enable increased stability and help to avoid painful wrists and are available in most computer shops.

- Place the screen on a lower table, in eye line, using another table at the right height for the keyboard, mouse or peripherals.
- Place the keyboard, rollerball and switch on a wheelchair tray with the screen on a table in front, at eye height.

Simple ideas to solve computer positioning problems

- Ensure that the chair is the right height for the table. Use chair risers if it is too low.
- Use an adjustable footrest if necessary or a pile of old telephone directories taped together.
- Angle the keyboard with the feet under the keyboard or place the keyboard on an angleboard with non-slip matting underneath.
- Stick upper or lower case letter stickers on the keys to aid pupils with visual impairments.
- Place the keyboard on a lap tray (tray with a beanbag underneath) with a piece of non-slip matting under the keyboard to stop it slipping.
- Use a keyguard to stop unwanted presses.
- Attach switches, joysticks and rollerballs to a piece of strong card or perspex with Velcro and fix it to the table or wheelchair tray with Blu-tak. Mark the exact location to ensure that switches are always in the right position for the individual. Alternatively, a Maxess tray and switch mounts can be used to position peripherals accurately and easily.
- Make cardboard overlays to access specific letters or keys for specific software as described in chapter 7.

What is a peripheral?

These are devices which enable access to the computer without using the keyboard or mouse.

- Switches can be activated in many different ways by touching, hitting, sucking, blowing, blinking or tilting. They can be tiny or huge, enabling people with the most severe motor difficulties to access the computer. They cannot be used to access all software, and require specialist software specifically written.
- Rollerballs are basically upside-down mice. The cursor is moved on the screen by moving the ball with a finger, toe or other part of the body. Different buttons carry out mouse functions or the ball can be used in conjunction with a switch, so that the cursor is moved by the rollerball and the switch activates the function.
- Special needs joysticks move the cursor around the screen in the same way as a computer game joystick. Introduce joystick software when introducing an electric wheelchair, as this helps the pupil's understanding of direction.
- Concept keyboards are touch-sensitive pads which send words, sounds and pictures to the computer by a single press. Overlays can be bought or made on any subject and programmed into the computer. Keyguards stop unwanted presses.
- IntelliKeys are a step up from concept keyboards, but work in the same basic way. Instead of having to load each individual overlay, as with the concept keyboard, there is a barcode on each overlay. As the overlay is placed on the board the correct overlay is automatically loaded. Software which runs with an ordinary keyboard will work with IntelliKeys. New overlays can be made with software called 'Overlay Maker' and keyguards are available to stop unwanted presses.
- Touch screens move the cursor as the finger is drawn across the screen. They are particularly useful for small children and can work with a fist as well as a finger. Pupils with motor difficulties may have

difficulties reaching out for any length of time. Most touch screens are attached to the monitor with Velcro, but there are now monitors with an integral touch screen.

- Keyboards come in all shapes and sizes including tiny, laptop-size and enlarged keyboards which plug into the computer in the normal way, QWERTY and alphabetical or specialist keyboards. A keyboard removes the need to plan the shape of each letter, so that the pupil can concentrate fully on the content of the writing.
- Infra-red devices are worn on the head, and move the cursor on the screen. A small infra-red receiver is placed on the computer and there are no wires.

Computers can give valuable access to all pupils and some software is equally appropriate for all pupils. Software which can be accessed by mouse, switches and other peripherals can be used by everyone. Unfortunately the majority of software cannot be accessed by people unable to use a keyboard or mouse, although accessible software is becoming much more available. This is a specialist area with too few people with sufficient experience and knowledge to advise the ever-increasing numbers of schools needing support.

Choosing appropriate software

- Choose software which can be accessed by the individual via switches and other peripherals if necessary.
- Consider voice-activated software such as 'Dragon dictate' which enables the user to control the computer with hands free. 'IBM VoiceType' is a dictation system only for word processing.
- Speech output software is extremely useful.
- Specialist centres can give advice. General ICT advisors are unlikely to have enough knowledge in this very specialist field.
- Where possible, use software which is accessible and appropriate for the whole class.
- Software such as 'Texthelp' will enlarge print and most word processors have large, clear fonts.
- Try out predictive software such as 'Prophet', 'Penfriend' and 'Texthelp'. These cut down the number of keystrokes required.
- Try onscreen keyboards such as those in 'Clicker', 'Point' and 'WiVik'.
- There are many graphic software packages with Clipart covering many topics for adults and children.

There is some very good software available for switch users, too many to list in this book. However, 'Clicker' software (Crick Software Ltd) stands out as an extremely good all-rounder, for those with learning difficulties, physical and sensory difficulties and for pupils of all ages in mainstream and special schools (see Appendix 14 for address). It runs on PC, Apple Mac and Archimedes and can be accessed with a mouse, switch or other peripheral. 'Clicker' creates a grid which can be of any size, made up of boxes or cells. This works on top of a word processor, sending words, symbols, numbers, sounds or pictures to the word processor, to be printed at the click of a button. All the computer function keys can be accessed by switches if needed and font size is easily changed. 'Clicker' speaks, using digitised voice or real voice via recorded sound files. Different packs are available to buy, but it is quick

Clicker software

and easy to create grids to meet the needs of the individual child and can be used at home and school. Mouse and switches can be permanently plugged in via a switch box to enable access for all. 'Clicker' grids can be swapped as long as both parties have bought the program.

- Liaise and plan grids with other schools to build up very good, cheap resources.
- Make photocopies of blank grids and write on these to design new grids.
- Train adults or older pupils to make the grids designed by the teacher.
- 'Clicker' can print off grids to be kept as a library and stored by topic, then grids can be viewed without turning on the computer.

Virtual therapy

Advanced Rehabilitation Therapies (ART) has been exploring the use of virtual reality for physical therapy and wheelchair training to increase the level of independence of disabled people. It was initially created to assist children with cerebral palsy to control a powered chair, but the product has a wide variety of uses. A 3D headset and joystick are used to move the user through various 3D environments. These products were developed by Dean Inman and David Warner from the Institute of Interventional Informatics (VNU Business Publications 1998). More information can be obtained from Advanced Rehabilitative Technologies (see Appendix 8 for details).

Internet, E-mail and the World Wide Web

E-mail is a way of communicating with people all around the world using the computer, a modem and a telephone line. An Internet Service Provider (ISP) is also required at a cost of approximately £10 per month. The modem plugs into the computer and when switched on uses the telephone to communicate messages to and from other computers. Schools using signs and symbols software can 'surf the net' enabling pupils to communicate with other symbol users across the world. The National Grid for Learning states that by the year 2002 all schools, colleges, universities and libraries will be connected to the Grid and 75 per cent of teachers and 50 per cent of pupils will have e-mail addresses. This will enable pupils with physical difficulties to 'travel' and communicate with the world for the price of a local telephone call. However, training is again likely to be an issue, to ensure access and equality.

The Computability Centre and the British Computer Society Disability Group, with funding from Microsoft, are developing an AbilityNet Web site. The aim is for the Web site to be fully accessible by Internet surfers with a wide range of disabilities. The Web site will mainly concentrate on enabling technologies and will provide information to keep people up to date with developments.

Chapter 9

Accessing the curriculum with pen/cil and paper

Pupils with severe motor difficulties may require a different approach to learning to make marks or write. They may need to use technology as their main means of recording, but it is also vital to extend fine motor skills to enable an alternative means of recording. This will require a well-planned programme, devised by teachers and occupational therapists together, incorporated into the curriculum.

Independent pen/cil skills can take a long time to acquire, but those achieved independently are internalised skills enabling children to have a greater degree of independence in the curriculum and in their future lives. Use of pen/cil and paper is a complex subject involving perception, fine and gross motor skills and many other skills.

The first marks a child makes on paper are likely to be circular scribbles and it is very important to encourage confidence and develop these skills. However, it is difficult for teachers to use scribble as a means of recording. This chapter describes how to develop greater accuracy in pen/cil skills to enable them to be used as a reliable means of recording. Some pupils may never be able to write functionally, but may eventually succeed in signing their name, which is a valuable life-skill.

The ability to hold a pen or pencil and make voluntary marks on a specific area of paper enables a person to record and communicate independently, without the need for speech. It needs no one else to be there, to listen or to make an immediate response. It is a powerful tool which is not generally utilised to its potential for children with severe motor difficulties. In the classroom it enables pupils to record their work independently and provides good evidence of a pupil's cognitive abilities, enabling teachers to plan appropriate access to the curriculum.

Why pen/cil and paper?

A pupil who has been taught the skills of marking will have a greater choice and will not be totally reliant on the computer, technology or an amanuensis.
The pupil will require the ability to:

Skills needed to make marks with a pen/cil

- hold a pen/cil the right way up with sufficient power to maintain position
- move the hand/arm voluntarily across the paper
- see where to mark
- make a mark on the paper at a designated place or area
- lift the pen/cil off the paper.

It is vital to involve the occupational therapist in assessing the best seating and positioning for each pupil, as this is crucial for the success of pen/cil and paper activities. *The pupil must be in a position to allow*

Seating and positioning to use pen/cil skills

optimum use of their hands, fingers and upper torso. The table or tray should be at the right height and use of an angle board may be necessary. Standing might be the most appropriate position for some pupils. Paper should be placed and angled in the correct position. Placing the paper on a piece of non-slip matting will stop the paper slipping; alternatively Blu-tak, masking tape or a magnet board can be used. Care must also be taken to ensure that the colour of the paper is appropriate for the pupil's vision and that the pencil requires little pressure.

Pens and pencils

- Always liaise with the occupational therapist when choosing appropriate tools and materials.
- Consider which pen/cils are most appropriate for the pupil.
- Collect a selection of felt-tipped pens and liaise with the occupational therapist.
- Try thick and thin chalks, oil or chalk pastels and art shop materials.
- Make a collection of oil pastel, chinagraph, coloured and EE pencils which require very little pressure.

Start by letting the pupil experiment with various mediums either independently or with an adult placing their hand over the child's to facilitate drawing lines, circles and letters. Every child is different, and some will need experience at this stage for some considerable time, but care must be taken not to stay at this stage for too long and they should be encouraged to draw independently. When the pupil can hold a pen/cil and make a mark independently, they are well on the way to success.

Pen/cil grips

- Commercially-available grips make pen/cils easier to hold.
- Pupils who cannot use a conventional grip might succeed with a specialist grip commercially available from specialist catalogues.
- Pupils should be able to hold objects of a variety of sizes before starting with pen/cil and paper. Being able to hold a ball the size of a tennis ball is sufficient to use the first pen/cil grip.
- Grips can also be made using various balls such as soft, squashy, polystyrene, bouncy, tennis, foam balls and golf practice balls.
- Make a ball pen/cil grip by pushing the pen/cil through a ball and winding a thick rubber band from the top of the pen/cil, over the ball and round the bottom of the pen/cil to prevent it slipping. Make sure there is enough pen/cil at the tip so the pupil can see the marks being made (see Figure 9.1).
- Over time and with success, gradually reduce the size of the ball. Regular pen/cil grips may now be appropriate and can be bought from various catalogues.
- Specialist tubing grip is available for different thickness of pen/cils or foam pipe cladding from DIY shops can be used. The foam should be cut to size and rubber bands used to anchor it to the pen/cil. This can also be used on paint brushes, cutlery and other handles.
- Grips can also be made from a specialist mouldable putty, which dries hard to the exact shape required.
- Some pupils are able to use a pen/cil in a palmar grasp. The pen/cil is pushed through a hole drilled in a piece of dowelling to make the

shape of a 'T' and a rubber band wound round the pen/cil and dowel to secure it (see Figure 9.2). The pupil holds the dowelling in the palm of their hand and moves the pen/cil. Although this allows the pupil to make marks on paper, it is very difficult to be accurate, and may be more suitable for art work.

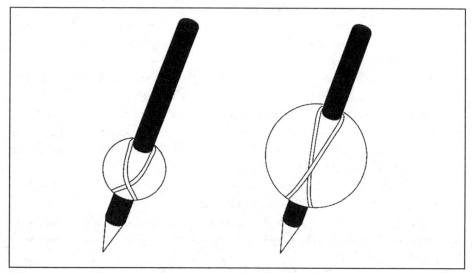

Figure 9.1 Gradually reduce the size of the ball on the pencil grip

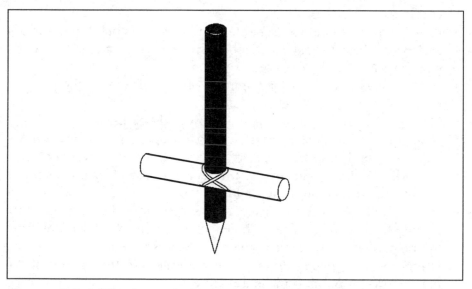

Figure 9.2 A 'T' grip made from wooden dowel and a rubber band

- Pupils need lots of practise to hold the pen/cil at the right angle with the tip on the paper, and to understand the relationship of their movements to the marks on the paper.
- Pupils should make dots, scribbles, short and long lines at different angles on the paper and need to learn to stop when asked. This involves lots of language and concepts such as short, long, straight, wiggly, spotty, left and right.
- Pupils should scribble independently (although you may not want to call it scribble). Singing to the movement of the pen/cil, e.g. round and round and round and round to the tune of 'Pop goes the weasel' involves a multi-sensory approach, helping the body to memorise movements and concepts.

Accessing the curriculum by marking with a pen/cil

Examples of how to use lines, dots and 'scribbles' in the curriculum

- Read the story of the book *Mr Messy* and cut out paper in the shape of Mr Messy, making it into a book.
- Establish good record-keeping by using each facing, blank page as a record sheet or photocopy a separate record sheet and store at the back of the book. Every piece of work requires a date, help given and a record of concepts achieved.
- Ask the pupil to 'colour' Mr Messy (in a flowing scribble action). Teach, match and consolidate colours, limiting the colours to one or two, adding one more with success.
- Introduce numbers 1 and 2, different shapes, body image and concept of happy or sad by using self-adhesive shapes of different colours. Look at faces, counting the number and colour of eyes.
- Add eyes using self-adhesive stickers of different colours and shapes.
- Draw a mouth on a self-adhesive strip for the pupil to place establishing whether Mr Messy is happy or sad.
- Make different books, for example, the Teletubbies, Tutankhamun, shape books or covering any class topic.
- Books can be lent or made for younger children or kept to establish a library. Older pupils can enjoy this activity if it is presented in a mature way.
- These pictures may also be scanned and turned into computer graphics, which can later be used in writing stories and books on the computer.
- Progress from free-flow (scribble) activities to short, long, straight and wavy lines to make hedgehog spines, long, straight, or curly hair, beards or bars on a cage.
- Make a zoo book by sticking animals on a page, asking the pupil to draw the bars on the cages.
- Make a face book with a variety of hair and beards.

Placing scribbles, lines and marks more accurately on the page

- When pupils are able to scribble and make lines and dots on the page voluntarily and when asked, they need to work towards placing the marks more accurately on the page. This will enable them to record the curriculum using multiple choice.
- Many pupils are able to make marks on paper, but cannot stop, ruining their work or making holes in the paper. Work on this from the beginning with a reward chart or stickers for success.
- Using A3 or A4 paper, draw or stick one item in the middle of the paper. Ask the pupil to make a mark on or by this, with a coloured felt-tipped pen. With success, gradually move the shape to the top, bottom or sides of the paper, making sure there is only one shape on each piece of paper. A topic-based picture, number, letter or shape should be used.
- With success, fold the paper in half and open out following the same procedure in each half.
- With success, fold the paper into quarters, then sixths, following the same procedure.
- With success, the pupil should now be able to mark on A4 paper, folded in half vertically and quarters or sixths horizontally, which is a useful size for differentiation and recording.
- Care must be taken to ensure success at each stage. The pupil may have difficulties due to a number of reasons, such as visual acuity or perceptual difficulties, as well as fine motor difficulties.

- A clear record of the pupil's abilities to mark on paper is required to ensure that the curriculum is differentiated appropriately.
- There is no reason why the pupil cannot record the curriculum while moving towards greater accuracy on paper.
- Important learning concepts should be differentiated according to the level of accuracy the pupil *can* already achieve to ensure that the pupil is able to concentrate on the curriculum, rather than use of pen/cil.
- Multiple choice can be used to access all areas of the curriculum, at any level.

- The ability to join items such as letters, words, phrases, and numbers introduces a new dimension to independent access, while also extending pen/cil skills. Use of lines consolidates and teaches directionality, introducing language and understanding of concepts such as 'to the top', 'across the page', 'to the right/left'. These skills are necessary when using a joystick to control an electric wheelchair, a toy or the cursor on the computer and for geography and general laterality.
- It is a much more natural movement to pull the arms towards the body, than to push away. Start with lines from top to bottom and from across the body to midline. As soon as the pen/cil has to be pushed, control may be lost.
- Ensure the pupil has the concept of 'same', practising activities with real objects and pictures, consolidated in daily activities at home and school. Ensure that pictures are appropriate for the pupil's age and for those with visual difficulties.
- Start by joining two identical items, such as their name, a letter, picture or number. One at the top of the paper and one directly underneath at the bottom (see Figure 9.3). Record understanding of different words and concepts, as they are introduced, to build an accurate picture of the pupil's cognitive and linguistic skills.

Using lines to join items

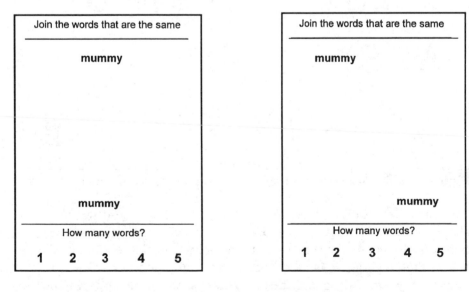

Figure 9.3 Join from top to bottom

Figure 9.4 Move the words to one side

- When the pupil can successfully link two items with a free-drawn line, move both items slightly to the side, the top to the right and the bottom to the left. To join the items the pupil must now draw a line at a small angle (see Figure 9.4).
- With success increase the angle of the line.
- Draw lines from top to bottom, at all angles, then introduce lines from left to right (not right to left) following the same model as from top to bottom. Over time, the pupil will be able to draw lines at any angle on the page.
- A4 paper can be cut in half and, with success, in half again. This reduces the size of the lines more to letter size.
- The pupil may now have the prerequisite skills for writing letters involving straight lines such as:

A E F H I i K k L l M N T V v W w X x Y Z

- When pupils start to write letters, it is extremely important to ensure success. Start with the word and capital letter I, reading and writing it throughout the school day. With the success of I, add T, then F and continue to add one more letter at a time. Letters such as A, V, W, X, Y and Z have diagonal lines which change direction, and these are extremely hard for some pupils to write.
- Teach recognition of upper- and lower-case letters, their names and phonic sounds *at the same time,* e.g. 'Its name is ess and it says sssss'.

This is a good time to find the same letters on a keyboard. If the keyboard is too confusing make a cardboard overlay and fix on top of the keyboard. Cut holes in the card corresponding to the letters being learnt it (see Figure 9.5). With success, cut more holes to access more letters. Keyboard overlays can also be made to access specific software or the pupil's name.

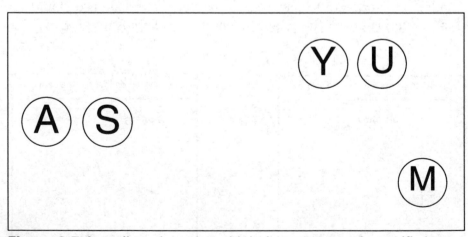

Figure 9.5 A cardboard overlay with holes cut to match specific letters

Going over dots or between lines to make letters and shapes

This is a very different technique from drawing free-flow lines and shapes. The pupil may be so concerned about keeping on the dots or between the lines, that they do not internalise the shape and flow of the letter. This technique is often used to teach young children to form letters. However, these activities may not be the most appropriate way to teach pupils with severe motor difficulties how to write letters or numerals. Able-bodied pupils use their eyes and senses, and by repetition of movement, their bodies learn the shape of the letters, enabling them to write letters independently. This learning process is likely to be different for pupils with motor difficulties, because of their physical limitations and need for adult facilitation, making them more likely to be passive learners, lacking independence and unable to consolidate learning in the same way as their able-bodied peers. Pupils in this situation are likely to 'switch off'.

Chapter 10

Reading. If I can read I can ...

Reading is a lifeline

The written word and speech are the two main ways that people communicate today. Reading is a lifeline to the world and society and for many children with severe motor difficulties it is an achievable goal which may not have been reached because of lack of expertise and training. Many children whose motor difficulties occur as a result of degenerative conditions or following an accident learn to read in the same way as their peers, but those who may also have hidden handicaps such as visual, perceptual or motor coordination difficulties, vision and hearing difficulties, epilepsy other complex needs are likely to have difficulties with reading. These more complex children need the support of the whole team to enable SENCOs and teachers to devise reading programmes to meet their individual needs. In the past, teachers have been constrained in the way they teach reading, but these constraints need to be removed. Pupils with disabilities who achieve a good level of communication and literacy have a better chance of inclusion at secondary school level.

Reading is often a major problem which worries parents, child and school alike. Schools may feel that their success in teaching able-bodied pupils to read enables them to teach a pupil with severe motor difficulties successfully in the same way. In some cases, this is the right thing to do, but in many cases the reading programme is inappropriate, requiring adaptation to meet the specific needs of the individual. Teaching reading to pupils with severe motor difficulties often challenges established practices. Teachers may be concerned that they do not have enough time to devise a reading programme for one pupil, but there is no reason why an adapted programme cannot be used by other pupils in the school. New national guidelines allow teachers more time to spend on developing the teaching of reading. Linking and sharing experiences and resources with other schools in the same position is very beneficial.

Assessment of need

The more obvious difficulties, such as visual acuity and hearing, may already have been diagnosed, but it is vital to ensure that the child has a full assessment by appropriate therapists, psychologists and doctors to establish other difficulties. Early referral and assessment enables early intervention; assessments should be ongoing, and in consultation with parents and school. The key to appropriate intervention is dependent on accurate interpretation of assessment, but for those complex cases there should be ongoing assessment and good recording of the child's abilities in functional situations by all members of the support team. Regular and effective liaison is crucial to ensure that teachers receive appropriate support and advice to plan and evaluate the reading programme.

Establishing a database of functional skills, concepts and abilities is a good starting point. Chapter 9 describes how to devise a programme to develop the use of pen/cil and paper, and the importance of recording everything the pupil can achieve in an easily accessible format. It is important to utilise and consolidate all the pupil's skills when planning a reading programme.

How do we learn to read and write?

Most children with severe motor difficulties have had very different early years experiences from their able-bodied peers and may not have been able to internalise concepts such as direction, shape, size, height, weight, because of their inability to explore the environment and objects. This affects their ability to learn; without independent mobility and fine motor coordination, they are unable to consolidate their learning in the same way as able-bodied peers unless specific activities are devised to achieve this. When a new letter, word or number is introduced, they are dependent on visual memory. Imagine learning to read and write a different script such as Arabic or Hebrew without being able to write! Learning would be completely dependent on visual memory, necessitating other strategies to help consolidate learning.

Creating an individualised reading programme

In this book I have used certain words, but there is no set list of words which is required, as long as the entire reading, writing and spelling programme is based around the *same words*. It is important for the child to make sense of them individually and when put together to form a short phrase or sentence. The words chosen should be heavy-duty words in common use with some names, characters and nouns, possibly linked to a reading scheme. With success, adjectives and adverbs can be added. Careful choice of words, materials and games ensures that materials are age appropriate. The aim is for the pupil to:

- recognise key words using a whole-word approach
- recognise the key words by their initial phonic sounds
- recognise keyword families
- recognise the names and phonic sounds of the letters making up key words
- recognise lower-case and capital letters of key words
- understand the meaning of the words individually and in a short phrase or sentence
- be able to use picture and other clues to help reading.

Consolidating key words, letters, names and sounds

The most crucial component for a successful literacy programme is for the pupil to be able to consolidate learning by *using* the key words daily, at every opportunity in and out of class, at home and school. Key words should be used in recording the curriculum, included in games and read in many different contexts. It is vital to devise specific activities requiring 'marking' and without the need to write, as described in Chapter 9.

Pupils should be able to recognise and use the words and letters:

- in a variety of contexts on flashcards, in books, with different sized and coloured print, written by hand and printed, in games, on worksheets, using an onscreen grid such as 'Clicker' (Crick Software Ltd), concept keyboard overlays and card readers which read and record cards. These have a protected master track and a student track to record;

- by 'writing' and spelling words in short phrases and sentences via computer keyboard, onscreen keyboard, computer software, read and stick and self-adhesive stickers, highlighting or joining words or letters with a pen/cil, using a magnetboard, dictation and recording on a tape recorder;
- to create new words using word families, e.g. c**at**, f**at**, h**at**.

Limit the words and letters

Plan approximately twenty key words to be read including approximately six high-interest nouns and four names or characters. An example of key words chosen:

can	I	am	is	has	a
in	the	likes	on	cat	dog
house	teddy	van	tree	mummy	daddy
Pat	Sam				

- The pupil should start by playing games as described in Chapter 7 to recognise their own name, as a word and as individual letters, with the addition of *one other word* from the list starting with a different letter, e.g. Sam, likes.
- When the pupil can consistently recognise both words, introduce *one more word*.
- With consistent success, introduce one more word at a time, ensuring that the core words are retained and understood and the pupil is able to use them in the curriculum and can read them in a variety of contexts.
- Choose key words which make short phrases or sentences when put together with a noun, e.g. I am Sam, I can see mummy, Mummy likes Sam.
- Write the words in short sentences introducing non-key words with a picture clue, e.g. mummy has a computer (picture of computer).
- Introduce questions, e.g. Can I see mummy? Am I a tree?

Use of pen/cil to consolidate reading

- *Marking/highlighting, joining with a line and multiple choice* are described in Chapter 9 and are ways of consolidating learning, as well as using technology.
- Make similar worksheets for each letter, word, phrase and word family.
- Mark, highlight or draw a line to join each word or letter.
- The first worksheets should start with the first two key words and their letters, adding one more with success. Limit the words and letters on a page.
- Letters and words should be of different sizes, with different print placed in different areas on the paper.
- Use a coloured pen to mark all the words that say, e.g., 'am' (Fig. 10.1).
- Join letters to a word family to make a new word (Fig. 10.2).
- Mark words in a specific word family (Fig. 10.3).
- Join or mark capital letters to lower-case letters and vice versa (Fig. 10.4).
  Repeat and consolidate these reading worksheets for use with:

- card reader
- concept keyboard

- onscreen grid using the 'Clicker' program
- touch screen.

Good record-keeping is essential to ensure that the teacher knows what the pupil can achieve, to enable them to plan the curriculum appropriately.

Figure 10.1 Find all the words that say 'am'

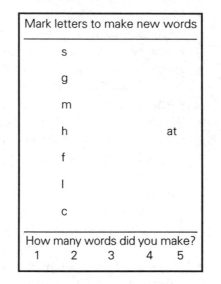

Figure 10.2 How many words can you make?

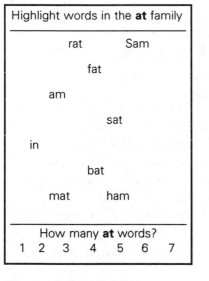

Figure 10.3 Highlight words in the 'at' family

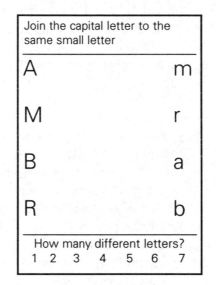

Figure 10.4 Join the capital letter to the same small letter

The word chest for reading and writing

The word chest consolidates reading, assesses reading abilities and ability to order words enabling pupils to write. Children often put words in the wrong order when first learning to write. Pupils with motor difficulties may have difficulties ordering words if they do not have the opportunity to practise. Ordering whole words is a speedy way of 'writing', releasing time to be spent on other related tasks.

- A small chest of plastic drawers is required.
- Photocopy key words, cut to the same size, storing a different word in each drawer and labelling each drawer clearly.

- Words can also be written on self-adhesive stickers and used in the same way.
- Cut small, blank pieces for spaces between the words. These can also be used to write new words.
- Place the individual drawers containing the known key words on the table, so that the pupil can choose words, sticking them on to paper in the word order they require.
- Staple approximately ten of the same words together to make a small book. These are easier to handle and can be placed on the table without the drawer.
- Words and booklets can also be stored alphabetically, in plastic wallets normally used to store business cards, postcards or small slot-in photograph albums. Only known key words should be used without picture clues, to ensure success and consolidation. Do not use many words which the pupil cannot read, as this will make the task unachievable. The main aim is to practise reading and, using the key words from the curriculum, to consolidate learning.

The spelling, maths and language chests

- Make a letter chest or plastic wallet in the same way as the word chest, using the letters to build words.
- Make a number chest to order numbers and to record maths, e.g. 2 + 3 = 5.
- Include mathematical shapes.
- Make a French, German, Hebrew chest to read, write and order words in different languages.
- Include word families in the letter chest, so that different initial letters can create new words, e.g. **S**am, **h**am.

Make a colour and black and white picture library

- Pupils who are unable to draw pictures for themselves can use pictures from the picture library to illustrate their work.
- Use plastic A4 size wallets in a ring binder, and label.
- Cut out pictures from magazines, catalogues and old books and store in categories such as animals, people, clothes, allowing the pupil a choice of pictures to illustrate their work.
- Keep the picture library well stocked. The whole class may help at wet playtimes! Magazines such as the National Geographic are excellent sources of good quality pictures and can often be found in charity shops.
- Build up a collection of computer graphics, print out and file by category with the filename on the computer. A scanner might also be used for pictures.
- Collect and file black and white pictures in the same way. These have the added advantage that they can be coloured, allowing a greater degree of independence and giving the pupil ownership of their picture.
- Access to a colour printer is important for pupils who are unable to draw recognisable pictures. Young children often colour pictures inappropriately, such as blue for a person's face. Children with motor difficulties need to go through the same learning processes.
- Pictures can be collected from photocopiable sheets, free drawing, line drawings or tracings; and photographs often photocopy well.
- Black and white pictures also enable teachers and assistants to create

work sheets and concept keyboard overlays in a matter of minutes and they photocopy well.

Ongoing liaison with parents is very important, so that they are involved and fully aware of the reasoning behind the choice of books and happy to give their support. In a mainstream school there is no reason why the usual reading scheme books cannot also be used, in parallel with an individual programme, as long as the pupil's own individual reading needs are also met.

Parents should understand which book the child should read *on their own* and which book parents should *read to them*. Pupils have full, consistent support when home and school are working together, helping them gain confidence and self-esteem as they learn.

Involve parents from the beginning

Finding enough books with the right sized print, the right number of words on a page with clear pictures, at an appropriate age level, is very difficult.

Where do I find enough books?

- Build up a collection of books which have the key words you have chosen, storing all the books with the same key words in the same zipper wallet. Look in school reading schemes old schemes, shops and jumble sales and ask parents.
- Label each book and zipper wallet with the key word.
- Ask neighbouring schools to help and join forces in sharing books, concept keyboard overlays, clicker grids and worksheets, benefiting children with reading difficulties in different schools.
- Recycle old books with missing pages by writing simple key word sentences on paper stuck over the print.
- Make mix-and-match books by making a book cut in half with a picture at the top and writing at the bottom. Mix up the pages, so the pupil has to match the writing to the correct picture.
- Make games, activities and books using photographs.
- Photocopy and make up books using the picture libraries and the computer. Some books should be made with different sizes and colours of print or written by hand.
- Replicate books with an onscreen grid or concept keyboard overlay, enabling the pupil to rewrite the book quickly and easily.
- Make card reader letters, words, phrases and word families.
- Introduce 'yes' and 'no' by making nonsense books, where the picture does not match the words.
- Make flip books from ordinary blank exercise books cut in half. Make sure there are not too many pages. Fold each page over into the centre. Write a word or phrase on top of the folded-over page and add a matching picture on the inside. The pupil opens out the page to self-correct.
- Start a keyword library by making books and collecting appropriate commercially available books from various schemes. Copy and share books with other schools.

Use your collection of small, real objects to make reading games as described in Chapter 7.

Games to include reading and therapy

- **Initial sounds** – make cards for the letters in the key words, e.g. 'cat', 'mummy', 'am', and place in a box with a few objects starting with the same phonic sounds, e.g. cards with a, m, h, u, y, o, n, c and small objects or pictures such as **a**pple, **m**ug, **h**at, **U**mbrella, **yo**-yo, **o**range, **n**ail, **c**at. The pupil is asked to place the objects next to the card matching the initial phonic sounds. Cards and photographs may also be attached to blocks. The introduction of tongs, pegs, boxes or barriers, etc., will help to achieve therapy targets.

- **Reading words** – make the same game as above, using whole-word cards to match to objects or photographs. If photographs or pictures are used they should be attached to blocks, for ease of handling or to enable tongs to be introduced.

- **Reading short phrases** – the same game is made where an object or photograph matches a card with a short sentence or phrase, e.g. 'I am mummy'.

- **Match the sound** – the teacher throws a beanbag or ball to a pupil saying a key word. The pupil has to say a word starting with the same letter before the count of 5 or 10.

- **Isolating a finger** – can be introduced by using a magnetboard. Self-adhesive magnetic tape or magnets are attached to each card and object. Cards are placed on one side of the board and objects on the other. The pupil is asked to push the right object to the right initial letter and vice versa. Playing the game wearing a finger puppet will add interest.

- **In-the-bag tactile element** – use the same objects and letter cards from the boxes, but place them all together in a bag or box. The pupil pulls out objects and cards, matching initial sounds.

- **Introduce a speech therapy and tactile element** – one pupil has letter cards, face-down on the table and another pupil has the objects in a bag. The letter cards are turned over in turn and the pupil with the bag is asked to find an object beginning with that letter.

- **Use of two hands** – can be introduced using the same cards and objects by putting the cards in one box and the objects in another. Both boxes are held out or placed on either side of the pupil, who is asked to reach out and take an object and a card in each hand. If the word or letter matches the object they are kept out as in Snap. It is vital that the two arms are stretched out together.

- **Strengthening muscles and practising the action for scissor-cutting** can be achieved with the same cards and objects. Place the cards down on the table with the objects in a box. Using tweezers, teabag squeezers or tongs, ask the pupil to pick up the objects one by one, placing them next to the correct card.

- **Working towards independent eating** using a spoon can be introduced by placing the objects in a bowl with the cards face upwards, singly on the table. The pupil uses a spoon to lift out the objects and place them on the correct card.

- **Encouraging a pincer grip** – can be practised by sticking the cards in a large box with shallow sides, or on a tin tray held down by magnetic strips in the shape of a football team on the pitch. Each object is placed on the tray in turn and the pupil is asked to flick the object until it lands on the right card. This is a good game for two to play by sharing out the objects and taking turns to flick. Cards and objects are taken off with success and winner is the one with the most objects and cards.

- **Establishing body parts** – can be included by making an additional set of cards showing drawings of body parts such as nose, fist, elbow, hand. The words or letter cards are spread out and placed face-up on the table-top. The objects are shared between two players. Each player takes turns to turn over a body card, then, using that body part, tries to move the object onto the right card. Alternatively, a doll can be taken to bits and the body parts used to push the objects.
- **Establishing body parts and strengthening pincer grip** – can be included by using body-part cards. The cards are shared between the players and turned over in turn. The card is read and pegged to the appropriate body part on a teddy or soft doll. Word cards can be attached to pegs with string.

All games can be adapted with a little ingenuity and thought; class teachers must remember that they are not therapists, but it is very important to plan and discuss ideas with therapists. Class teachers are expert in the field of education and, in partnership with therapists, each can learn from the other. These are just a few examples of how therapy can be included in the reading programme, but the same principle applies for all curriculum areas. Be adventurous and make sure that the pupil, parents and therapists know what is being covered. Above all it should be *fun and achievable*. Cognitive and therapy aims should be carefully graded to ensure success. Consolidation is required for therapy in the same way as it is for learning, but care must be taken to ensure that the therapy part of the game is not too hard for the individual. Therapy aims should be tailored to the individual and not be allowed to dominate what is essentially a learning game.

Use your imagination

Chapter 11

Maths and science – will my chair fit in your lunchbox?

Maths is more than numbers!

Mathematics is about numbers, patterns, sequences, size, shape and their relationships and a hundred other things. Young children learn about many mathematical elements by exploring the world around them. They feel shapes in their mouths, explore what will and will not fit into things and begin to see relationships between objects. They may not know what two is, but they can certainly estimate that two is more than one. Offer a young child one or two sweets and the chances are that they will take the two! Mathematical language is matched to concepts such as 'more than', 'biggest' and 'same as'. When children start school at the age of four or five, they are already equipped with a lot of mathematical knowledge and language.

Difficulties with visual and auditory memory, perceptual skills and attention have crucial effects on mathematical abilities. Pupils may have difficulties remembering what they have been told to do, what they are doing, sequencing and ordering numbers, holding and remembering numbers and processing numbers in their head. A pupil who lacks attention and is unable to concentrate and stay on-task, makes lots of little mistakes. They may look away when counting, returning to count the wrong object or number or start to count something else altogether. This can sometimes be interpreted as the pupil 'being naughty'. In fact it is very hard for the pupil to stay on-task and they may need to be taught some key processes and strategies, one-to-one in a quiet area of the classroom or outside the class, enabling them to concentrate without distraction. Some people feel that this is not good practice for inclusion, but inclusion is also about meeting individual needs. This would be included in the pupil's IEP and reviewed regularly.

Practical maths – counting objects and counting on paper

It is important for pupils to use concrete objects and mathematical apparatus, such as unifix cubes or magnetic blocks, to help them understand mathematical concepts, regardless of how slow they might be. It is easy for the adult to 'take over', but it is important that pupils learn by their mistakes, as well as by their successes. A pupil may count concrete objects, as part of an occupational therapy exercise for a planned session recorded in the IEP, but access to main maths and counting exercises should be achieved using one apparatus the pupil is best able to handle, possibly with manual facilitation. Some pupils may find apparatus very difficult to handle and sometimes it takes so long for the pupil to pick up the apparatus, they have forgotten what they are supposed to be doing with it. Choose or adapt apparatus to suit the individual and if use of one apparatus has failed, try another. Counting objects and many other maths activities involve an understanding of direction which is discussed in the geography section of Chapter 12.

Practical ideas to help with maths

- **Self-adhesive magnetic tape** can be attached to cubes and other apparatus, to enable the pupil to push them across a magnetboard, rather than pick them up for counting. This isolates the index finger, increasing dexterity and strength. It also avoids involuntary movements caused by reaching and grasping. Using objects linked to the curriculum to count introduces the language of that topic. These could be objects of different colours, shapes, sizes, farm animals or objects with different textures.

- **Abacuses** are commercially available and can be useful for some pupils, using the index finger to move the beads. There are often too many beads, but it is easy to make a simple abacus using large beads and thin wooden dowelling or coat-hanger wire. Beads are threaded onto the dowel which is glued into a square block at each end.

- **Photocopy and enlarge:** counting activities presented on paper should be the right size and quality for the pupil. Worksheets or paper should be designed to meet the pupil's needs or photocopied and enlarged to the right size, making sure that there is not too much on a page.

- **Counting with objects:** the pupil can place cubes or objects on top of each item to be counted on paper then taken off as they are counted. If the pupil loses count they may count the items in the container before continuing.

- **Marking/highlighting:** marking each item on the paper, as it is counted, avoids double counting and helps the pupil to re-count if distracted. Another colour should be used to re-count.

- **Not too much on a page:** if the pupil is expected to use a maths or work book for a specific reason, cover part of the page with a dark-coloured card to eliminate unwanted text. Alternatively cut a large rectangle out of a piece of dark card, creating a window for the task. Use paper clips or Blu-tak to anchor the card.

- **Estimating:** many pupils have difficulties counting, but are able to estimate quite well. Make sure pupils estimate before counting, so they can recognise if they have wildly miscounted.

- **Dice patterns:** numbers presented in the form of dice patterns are easier to count than those spread out in a line. The pattern provides a visual clue to the numbers. Children quickly recognise the number of dots on a dice, without having to count. This visual skill can be utilised in maths exercises. Practise using a dice in a variety of games

- **Strict counting rules:** pupils who are easily distracted need strict rules when counting. They should be brought back to task and not allowed to talk about unrelated subjects. Speech therapists can give hints and strategies to help staff handle this situation.

- **Functional counting:** counting should be introduced into the daily routine at every opportunity. Count buttons on clothes, wheels on a car, legs on a dog. Recognise numerals on car number plates and doors. Pupils should know that a dog always has four legs and a person has two legs. Counting can also be practised while doing physiotherapy stretches.

- **Spinner:** the spinner can be activated by a switch to give an element of chance in games. New overlays can be made for different games.

Understanding capacity, size and shape

Some pupils with motor difficulties have had few experiences of handling everyday objects, have little idea about size, shape and capacity and have missed out on the appropriate language and comprehension. Some pupils may also have difficulties with abstract thought and find it hard to predict what is likely to happen.

'Will my chair fit in your lunchbox?'

This activity can be introduced at odd moments of the day as part of an IEP. It is best played one-to-one with an adult for accurate recording, but can be played and recorded by small groups of pupils. It is important to start by using a container which the pupil knows well, such as their lunchbox. The game practises and assesses skills in language, comprehension, listening, visual spatial and perceptual abilities, measuring and capacity, abstract thought, and reach and grasp.

- An adult selects six to eight real objects, some which fit in the box and others which do not. These items should be linked to the topics in the curriculum or IEP targets and listed on one side of the record sheet (Figure 11.1).
- The pupil picks up and handles the box, which is then placed on the table.
- The objects are given to the pupil who names and briefly describes them one by one. This is recorded by an adult.
- Pupils guess whether the object will fit in the box. They should have no adult help and should not try to fit the object in the box at this stage.
- After naming all objects, they pick up each object in turn, try to fit it in the box themselves, and say whether it fitted and why.
- This activity enables the teacher/adult to have a clearer idea about the pupil's mathematical, visual spatial, perceptual and language abilities and, with accurate recording, to be able to pick out areas requiring further work. Liaison with the speech therapist is important, as they will be able to help interpret any difficulties and give advice. Using curriculum topic objects assesses whether the pupil can name them and consolidates topic language.

Extend the game

The game can be extended by changing the box and the objects and by introducing abstract thought and planning.

- Use different boxes, tins, baskets of different sizes, colours and shapes plus every day containers, such as washing-up bowls, pans, yoghurt pots and sweet jars.

- When the pupil has successfully experienced real objects, move to abstract thinking where the pupil has to imagine whether the object will or will not fit, e.g. 'Will a real bus fit in the hall?'
- Accurate record-keeping is vital for pupils with particular difficulties and over time builds a valuable record of their abilities and how the pupil is learning. A simple record sheet can be devised for groups of children to record themselves.

Record sheet for game	Will my chair fit your lunchbox?		
Name _____ Class _____			
Container chosen _____			
List of objects	will it fit?	did it fit?	Pupil's reasoning
1			
2			
3			
4			
5			
6			

Figure 11.1 'Will my chair fit in your lunchbox?'

Use of calculators

- There are many calculators on the market with large, clear numbers which can be used to check or calculate answers.
- Pupils should always read the numbers aloud to show they have understood. There is often confusion about the decimal point on the calculator display, so teach pupils early on that:

1 = 1.0 = 1.00
2 = 2.0 = 2.00 etc.

- It is useful for either adult and pupil or two pupils to compare answers and check for accuracy, giving the pupil confidence to work in pairs.
- Windows '95 and other applications have calculators already installed.
- A large onscreen, talking calculator called Big:Calc is available from Don Johnston (see Appendix 14 for address).
- Design-a-Calculator is a simple calculator which can be personalised, free on the Oxford ACE Centre's Web site.

Ordering numbers and counting

Counting and ordering numbers verbally and on paper can be very difficult for some pupils with severe motor difficulties and poor short-term memory. They may make errors in their responses, but may understand the concept in practical situations. It is important not to frustrate the pupil by holding them back until they reach 100 per cent accuracy. The teacher needs to establish the weaknesses and teach strategies to overcome them. The educational psychologist is an important member of the support team who can help teachers plan an appropriate maths curriculum for pupils with such difficulties.

Aids for counting and ordering numbers

- **Maths chest** – has been described in Chapter 10.
- **Number line** – on the pupil's desk, above the blackboard, below the computer monitor, on the keyboard, stuck on a ruler or on each page of maths work will help. Pupils should also be taught to use and recognise the numbers and their order on the computer keyboard, as soon as possible.
- **100 squares** – make a book of 100 number squares showing the multiplication table patterns. This visual representation reinforces learning.
- **Numerals on cards** – order numerals using magnetic letters or numeral cards attached to blocks or magnets.
- **Onscreen grids** – can be made to order numbers using mouse, switch, roller ball or other peripherals, recorded on a word processor and printed out.
- **Audio tapes** – counting in 1s, 2s, 5s, etc. can be practised by making or adapting a well-known tune. Multiplication music tapes are on sale or can be made by pupils in the class. Pupils can listen together or independently with a Walkman at home and school.
- **Card readers** – have a piece of audio tape attached to the bottom of the cards enabling the pupil to record their own voice or listen to the teacher's voice. Numbers can be written on the cards and recorded to practise counting and recognition. Real objects can also be stuck onto cards.
- **Concept keyboards** – can use printed numerals and real objects attached to overlays.

Mathematical equipment

Pupils with motor difficulties often have problems holding and using maths equipment. This need not be expensive and, in liaison with the occupational therapist, can be adapted by attaching knobs or handles. Specialist maths equipment can be bought from catalogues.

- Rulers can be adapted by screwing or gluing on handles or knobs and rested on non-slip matting.
- Money can be stuck onto small blocks of wood or foam to make the coins easier to pick up. A piece of magnetic tape enables them to be picked up using a magnet. Put coins in a small plastic pot with a lid to see both sides.
- Maths software for SEN and switch use are available from many catalogues.

Science

Many scientific skills and abilities are learnt in the early years in the same way as mathematical skills. Young children learn about the world by exploring and investigating the environment in a multi-sensory way. Pupils with severe motor difficulties have often missed out on this vital exploration, seriously restricting their perception of the world. Their understanding of space and development of mathematical and scientific language and concepts may be severely limited, which has important consequences for their learning. Science investigations involve observation, identifying, explaining, predicting and solving problems, developing strategies to deal with them and evaluating the results, which are important life-skills.

Planning

Science lessons require good planning, especially for pupils with severe motor difficulties. Pupils should be included in groups to be able to discuss, predict and experiment together. Planning will be required to:

- think about classroom management, moving furniture within the room to create more space to reach equipment and taps and sockets;
- liaise with teaching assistant to plan how support will be used;
- liaise with the occupational therapist to establish appropriate equipment
- adapt equipment or make sure that it can be used by the individual;
- ensure that activities, such as pulling, pushing and twisting, can be achieved in some way;
- consider health and safety and ensure that the pupil will have adult help
- ensure that teaching styles and recording cover special requirements such as perceptual or visual difficulties. Text might need to be enlarged or spaced out and record sheets devised to enable pupils to mark if necessary. This might be with a multiple choice answer, e.g.

When heated the chocolate went hard/melted/stayed the same.

Sensitive issues

A common theme in primary schools is the topic 'Ourselves'. This can raise sensitive issues and careful planning is required to ensure there is no embarrassment for any pupil in the class. Parents and the pupil should be consulted if any discussion about their disability is planned. Some families do not want their child to know too much about their disability, for whatever reason, and this should be respected, whatever the feelings of the school. However, this topic represents the opportunity to think about disability issues and problem solve, as a class, thinking of the best way to enable access and independence. It is surprising how even nursery children can identify the problems and solve them in a sensible way.

The game of sort and talk

This game can be included in science and considers attributes and categories. It can be played one-to-one with an adult or in a small group. It covers manual dexterity, fine motor control, perception, comprehension and use of language, abstract thought, observing, predicting and trying things out.

- The teacher chooses one category and writes this at the top of the sheet as Category 1. The second category is always the negative of the first category. This eliminates the need to comprehend more complex language, e.g:

  Category 1 – Floats   Category 2 – Does not float
  Category 1 – Is made   Category 2 – Is not made
          of metal   metal

- The teacher selects six to ten items, some which meet Category 1 and some Category 2. These are listed down the left side of the record sheet.

- The pupil picks up and handles each object in turn and decides whether it comes under the first or second category and this is carefully recorded. A pupil who can hold a pen/cil and mark can record this independently by ticking the box.

- When each object has been categorised, pupils should compare what they have written and establish whether they were right. They may need to experiment to find out the answer, e.g. it will float or not. Adult input is required to encourage pupils to give reasons and to mirror the correct use of language.

- Any category can be used, e.g:

  Shiny   – not shiny   Lives   – does not live
  Liquid   – not liquid   Wood   – not wood
  Will melt – will not melt   Solid   – not solid

- The same game can be played with categories in other curriculum subjects such as:

  Category 1   Category 2
  Found in space   not found in space.
  Victorian   not Victorian

Record sheet for game of **SORT and TALK**			
Name _____ Class _____			
Category 1 _____ Category 2 _____			
List of objects	Category 1	Category 2	Was I right? – Pupil comments
1			
2			
3			
4			
5			
6			

Figure 11.2 Example record sheet for SORT and TALK

Access to scientific equipment

- **The table or workbench** should be stable and resistant to quite high temperatures and household chemicals. Ideally, pupils with motor difficulties should sit around the table with their peers, but it is important to have the right height of table to accommodate wheelchairs. A group of pupils may work at a higher table if seating is found to enable them to work comfortably at a greater height. A tray may be attached to a chair or stander and placed where it allows the pupil to work within a group. Adjustable-height tables are commercially available to meet the needs of pupils with motor difficulties.

- **Sand and water trays** enable pupils to experience and explore the properties of sand and water. There are commercially available adjustable-height sand trays and also an hourglass-shaped tray which allows more access for pupils in wheelchairs. If these are not available, a small plastic tray can be placed on a wheelchair or standing frame tray with peers standing to join in. Alternatively, a tray can be placed on the floor and used with a floor sitter or adult support.
- **Large plastic aprons, tabards and wrist cuffs** should be available to cover the pupil, the tray and chair.
- **Non-slip matting** is plastic matting bought on a roll or as a mat which stops anything placed on top of it from sliding about. It can also be used to improve the grip on a container or to aid the removal of a lid. It can be cut to size and regular washing in warm, soapy water reinstates its 'sticky' properties.
- **Non-slip material** is valuable to stop larger objects, or people, from slipping. It is normally used to stop rugs from slipping on smooth floors and can be bought at carpet shops and IKEA.
- **Velcro** can be attached to items to fix them to work surfaces.
- **Blu-tak or plasticine** can be useful as a base to hold soft fruits or flowers by impaling them onto a cocktail stick set in the base. Cocktail sticks can also be set into small blocks of Plaster of Paris or wooden blocks.
- **Wood and nails** can be hammered through a piece of wood to allow objects to be impaled. Alternatively, a carving board or commercially produced gripper can be used.
- **Foam tubing** used to insulate pipes can be bought in DIY shops and cut to size to give added grip to utensils, rods and tubes.
- **Cup hooks** can be stuck onto items to make them easier to hold.
- **Tap turners** improve grip or leverage on taps and gas knobs.
- **Pouring liquids** in a kettle pourer avoids having to lift the kettle.
- **Feeding cups** can pour liquids, without the risk of spillage, when the holes are enlarged with a sharp knife or by burning with a heated knitting needle.
- **Measuring time** can be achieved by using electronic clocks and timers with large displays and control knobs.
- **Measuring weight** can be achieved by using electronic kitchen or bathroom scales for small and large items.
- **Measuring temperature** with electronic and liquid crystal thermometers, which consist of strips which change colour at different temperatures is less hazardous than using glass thermometers. Body temperature can be measured using a forehead strip thermometer, which can be bought at any chemist.
- **Measuring length** can be achieved with tape measures and rulers fixed with Blu-tak. Measure larger objects with Velcro sewn onto a material tape measure. The other side of the Velcro should be fixed to a large piece of strong cardboard.

- **Magnifiers** can be fixed on stands or on a flexible arm, as used in needlework. Small magnifiers attached to containers to view small creatures are useful. Sheets of plastic which magnify come in different sizes and are light and easy to handle, although the quality of the image is not as clear as with a conventional lens.

- **Microscopes** require fine adjustment and positioning and may not be suitable for pupils with severe motor difficulties. The binocular microscope avoids the need to close one eye to look down the microscope and produces a picture that is the right way round, rather than upside down. Microprojection is available to allow transparent objects and small creatures to be viewed on a screen or wall, using an attachment to a projector. Closed-circuit television (CCTV) enables pupils who may also have a visual difficulty to view small items.

- **Gardening tools** which are lighter with longer handles and therefore, more suitable for people with motor difficulties can be bought in local plant centres. Raised flowerbeds, using railway sleepers, tyres or log rolls purchased at garden centres, enable pupils to reach more easily. Ponds and environmental areas should have wheelchair access and thought should be given to safety and overall access.

- **Eye protection** should be adequate with safety glasses, but if they are likely to become dislodged, goggles can be fitted over the pupil's own spectacles. Pupils who cannot cope with goggles or glasses may need to use a face-shield or even sit behind a glass or plastic screen if toxic chemicals are involved.

- **Toys for science** can be found in most toy shops. Centres such as PLANET (Play, Leisure Advice Network) have many exciting, simple toys with ideas to make and buy. Many toys move, roll, balance, are wound up with keys to store energy or use battery or mains electricity, refract light such as kaleidoscopes, or can be electrically projected onto a wall. Battery toys can be accessed using a switch and a battery adapter available from various catalogues. A switch is attached to the toy, which is activated by the pupil pressing, pushing, hitting, blinking, sucking or blowing.

- **Electricity** is used by many pupils with severe motor difficulties in their wheelchairs, computers and electronic toys. Conventional electric circuit kits are too small and fiddly, but are available in large-scale versions which are fixed with Velcro.

- **Clamps and frames** hold objects safely for investigative work. A laboratory retort stand can be the frame to hold a variety of objects via clamps and clips. 'G' clamps can be used to fix stands and many other items firmly to the table top.

- **Experiments using open flames** can sometimes be replaced by using an electrical heater.

- **Scientific templates** are available to draw science equipment.

The classroom environment

- **Space** is probably the most important and difficult commodity to provide in the classroom, but with a little planning, common sense and ingenuity the environment can be made safe and practical.

Ideally lever taps and a sink with hot and cold water at the right height should be available. Commercially produced adjustable-height sinks are available. Pupils need to experience activities rather than being excluded because the environment is not perfect.

- **Electric socket extenders** should be at a height suitable for someone in a wheelchair. An extension socket can be fixed to the wall, ensuring that all cables are hidden and are not dragging on the floor. They should not be on the table-top if there is any chance of liquids being spilt.
- **Good lighting** is essential, particularly for pupils with any visual difficulty. An angled lamp can help to add direct light.
- **Displays and diagrams** should be able to be seen by a pupil in a wheelchair and not placed too high.
- **Storage** of the most commonly used items should be at wheelchair height. Other items may need to be fetched for the pupil or placed on a table at a suitable height to encourage independence.

The outdoor environment

The outdoor environment should not be overlooked and will require adaptations to allow access to those with walkers or wheelchairs. Paths should be wide enough to take a wheelchair and allow another person to pass. Architects and surveyors can advise on the correct gradients for slopes. There should be no obstacles or overhanging branches and it helps if there is an area with sufficient space for the wheelchair to turn; raised gardens and ponds allow further access to people in wheelchairs. Occupational therapists should always be involved with the planning of any adaptations, inside or out.

Chapter 12

Physical education, technology and geography

Physical education and games

Physical education (PE) is important for all children and especially for pupils with disabilities. Although their need is greater, they often have less opportunity to play and exercise than their peers. There are often fewer sporting opportunities for pupils with physical disabilities in mainstream schools, especially in secondary schools which focus on developing skills in particular sports. More pupils with severe motor difficulties are now included into mainstream schools and it is important to ensure that they are not being excluded from PE, dance and games lessons. Teachers face a challenge to include these children in normal lessons and to give them a range of activities which stretch them, but where they can achieve success.

Involving the physiotherapist and support team

Physiotherapists advise on appropriate physical activities, but when such advice is not available it is easy to see why teachers err on the side of caution. Teachers should feel that they have the support of other professionals to ensure individual needs are met. Therapists advise on the pupils' strengths and weaknesses and the medical team can ensure that staff are aware of any medical difficulties. As keyworker, the SENCO should be in a position to advise school staff. Class teachers and PE specialist staff will benefit from attending a physiotherapy session to observe what the pupil can achieve and, together with the physiotherapist, plan an individual physical activity programme to meet and challenge the pupil's short- and long-term needs. Class teachers should discuss all physical activity plans with the physiotherapist to ensure they are appropriate for individual pupils.

Questions teachers might ask the support team

- Should normal PE kit be worn and if not, what should be worn?
- Should splints, calipers and orthopaedic boots be removed?
- Is the pupil's condition likely to fluctuate or deteriorate in the lesson as a result of heat, cold or tiredness?
- Should the pupil have short rests between activities and if so, in what position?
- Are there any activities which should be avoided completely?
- Which types of activities are recommended?
- Should a wheelchair user stay in their wheelchair for all activities?
- Can the pupil transfer in and out of their wheelchair independently?
- Will the pupil require lifting onto specialist equipment for mobility?

- Are two people needed to lift and are they trained and available?
- If the teacher is likely to be the second person to lift, who will give appropriate training?
- Is the pupil on any medication which might affect performance?
- Is the pupil aware of their limitations or are they likely to be a danger to themselves and others? How should this be handled?
- Is the condition degenerative?
- Has the pupil got visual, hearing, perceptual or any other difficulties relevant to the activity?
- Does the pupil have a condition, such as epilepsy, likely to require support or an emergency procedure to be put in action?
- Are all school staff aware of the emergency procedure for an individual pupil?
- Is the pupil continent?
- Does the pupil need to wear glasses? Are the lenses plastic?
- Is the pupil colour-blind?

Ways of working

Physiotherapy targets may involve walking using a specialist walker, independent walking, standing independently or in a standing frame, sitting independently, standing from sitting or sitting from standing, rolling over, crawling, pushing or strengthening upper arms. Many of these targets can be incorporated into everyday activities and practised in PE lessons which can take different forms such as:

- **integrated sessions plus adult help** – working with peers on the same activities with adult helper to support and facilitate;
- **parallel sessions** – working alongside peers, but on different activities;
- **adapted sessions** – working alongside peers doing the same activity adapted to meet their needs;
- **alternative sessions** – in school working individually on a specific activity such as wheelchair practice, boules or specific movement sessions away from peers;
- **alternative sessions** – out of school going swimming or to an outside sports centre or joining a special school for some sports.

Alternative sports

There may be circumstances when it is not practical to include a pupil with disabilities. Contact and team sports such as hockey, cricket, football and rugby played on outside grass pitches do not lend themselves to inclusion, although pupils may want to be included as umpire or scorer. When activities cannot be suitably adapted, consideration should be given to using out-of-school facilities. It may be that a range of alternative activities need to be considered to provide a challenge and to develop enthusiasm for movement and a chance to enjoy and experience success. These might be riding, archery, weight training, sailing, canoeing or swimming. If pupils are to develop skills above a certain level, they require specialist coaching. Sailing or specialist clubs can be established including able-bodied and disabled pupils.

Swimming

Swimming is a hobby which people with disabilities can enjoy all their lives. It is an ideal sport, allowing freedom which pupils may only experience in the water. Movement of the body improves circulation and allows active and passive movements of joints to avoid contractures. Movement is more difficult in cold water, therefore the temperature of the water should be checked to avoid hypothermia. Pupils with limited mobility may be unable to right themselves in the water or feel the cold in paralysed limbs. It is very important to ensure that they are closely supervised and wear a swimming aid. 'Swimfriends' produce some specialist swimming aids which enable people to maintain a good body position in the water, so the pupil can be more independent and control their own movements, without hindrance. Buoyancy aids can also help people who cannot walk on land to walk in the water. Instructors should have the basic Instructor's Certificate and the Preliminary Certificate for Teaching People with Disabilities. All courses are registered with the Amateur Swimming Association who can advise on available suitable training around the country. A list of addresses is included in Appendix 12.

Training for physical education

The increasing numbers of pupils with disabilities included in mainstream schools means that training is urgently needed to ensure they have a broad and balanced curriculum, including PE, games and dance. It is important for new teachers to have appropriate teacher training, to know the capabilities and limitations of the major disabilities, how to adapt physical activities, how to work as part of a large support team for individual pupils and how to make physical activities accessible. Greater links and integration between special and mainstream schools should be established for the benefit of all pupils and staff. PE teachers in special schools could train, advise and work as peripatetic teachers across different schools, including mainstream. There is a need for specialist support teachers in PE, as well as maths and science and other curriculum areas.

Disability sports

It is well worth finding any disability sports clubs and forums in the locality. The London Sports Forum for disabled people is a registered charity and has published a booklet with 50 positive images of disabled people taking part in sports (see Appendix 12).

Good ideas to incorporate into PE

- **Stretching muscles** and gaining control of their movements can benefit all pupils. Physiotherapy stretches for some individual pupils with severe motor difficulties could be introduced as part of a general warm-up at the beginning of a lesson.
- **Involve older children or other adults** as partners for pupils with disabilities to facilitate and support movement and for the pupil to gain trust.

- **Pair up an able-bodied pupil** with a pupil with motor difficulties if it involves passing balls, as they require an accurately placed ball for success.
- **'Flower'** involves a pupil curling up as tightly as they can and a second pupil trying to open them out, while the pupil resists. This builds strength and helps with body awareness. Ask the pupils to name the parts of the body as they are opened.
- **Read and throw:** a word is held up and pupils throw a beanbag at the correct word on the floor. Use different coloured bags for individuals.
- **Count and throw:** a card with a number of items is held up for the pupil to count. The pupil then throw a beanbag at the corresponding numeral card on the floor.
- **Stick to the floor** involves the pupil lying as flat as they can on the floor on their back or tummy. A partner pretends to stick them to the floor, then tries to unstick parts of the body against resistance, naming body parts.
- **Back to back:** two pupils sit back-to-back and push against each other, although neither must be allowed to be rough.
- **Roll over** on the floor, taking turns to direct the other to roll to the left or to the right. Put a number, colour, word on the floor directing the pupil to roll to number 5 or left. This develops independence so the pupil can roll over in bed, aiding carers.
- **Obstacle course** involves pupils moving under, over, along or through a piece of equipment in different ways. This might include bottom shuffling, crawling (no bunny hops!), rolling, walking, backwards or forwards. Arriving at the obstacle, the pupil turns over a card with pictures or words directing them how to move to the next obstacle.
- **Wheelchair obstacle courses** are essential for wheelchair users to practise techniques to become really efficient.
- **Compensating movements** are required when the pupil sits on a wobble board or across a roll, trying to keep upright as it is moved from side to side.
- **'All change'** develops body image. Children move about the hall and when the teacher calls 'finger to finger' they must find a partner and put their fingers together. Any body parts can be used which two people can touch.
- **Bilateral pushing** involves two pupils sitting opposite each other, taking turns to push a large ball backwards and forwards to each other, using two hands together. Link it to the curriculum by introducing colour or a numeral card to direct the number of times it should be pushed and vary the size of the ball from huge to small. This activity practises tracking, anticipation, reach and grasp.
- **In the box (1)** involves the pupil throwing a beanbag into a box, marking where the pupil should stand or sit, repositioning with success. Start with four beanbags of the same weight, changing to different weights with success. Link this to the curriculum by changing the container and labelling it with words, numbers, colours, using language such as heavy, light, left and right, planning use of language beforehand.

- **In the box (2)** same as above, but the pupil stands or sits centrally with containers placed on either side and in front. The pupil throws a beanbag across their body. Left throw to right container and right throw to left container. A partner checks and records use of correct hand. Change the height, size, shape, colour of the container and the weight, colour, shape and size of the beanbags.
- **Doing two things at once** is difficult for some pupils. Ask them to clap hands, make a circle with their finger in the air or bang a drum, while answering simple questions such as 'What's your name?' The activity is likely to stop when concentration is needed for the answer.
- **Building upper arm strength (1)** involves the pupil sitting sideways on a bench with two hands flat at the sides. They lift their bodyweight with two arms moving along the bench, pushing with feet flat on the floor.
- **Building upper arm strength (2)** (stretching, resisting and body awareness) is achieved when the pupil lies along a bench stretching out arms full length and gripping the sides of the bench to pull or push themselves along.
- **Bilateral game** is when two balls or beanbags of the same weight are given to the pupil, one in each hand. Both bags are thrown into a box, directly in front of them, letting go at the same time, increasing distance with success.
- **Rhythm banging:** two things at once – can be part of the music or PE curriculum. The pupil is asked to say or sing a short phrase such as 'Three blind mice' and asked to bang a drum on the last word:

bang

Three blind **mice**. With success change the 'bang' word:

bang

e.g. Three **blind** mice

- **Beanbag golf** is played in pairs, each pair using different coloured beanbags. Place boxes, hoops, baskets and different sizes and shapes of containers around the hall on and under tables, mats, benches or high stools and under equipment, forming different targets. Scores are recorded as pupils move round and hit the targets. Different weighted beanbags makes this game much more difficult.
- **Pass the objects** is when the pupils sit in a small circle and two different objects are passed around, one going clockwise and the other anti-clockwise. Pupils are 'out' when they hold both objects. This practises grasp and release and crossing midline. Objects may be linked to the curriculum; two objects of very different sizes increases the difficulty.

Simple equipment to create and adapt physical activities

- **Guttering** can be bought in lengths from DIY shops and cut to size with a hacksaw. Games can be made particularly for pupils in wheelchairs, where balls are rolled down the guttering to knock something down or to land on a target. Pupils who are unable to direct the guttering may have a partner to do this. Different types and weights of balls roll at different rates and the height of the guttering influences speed. The game covers grasp and release, ability to aim, use of language, directing others, turn-taking and visual perception as well as curriculum targets included in the game.

- **Treasure Island** is a target game. An island is painted on an old sheet or paper and objects placed around the island. The ball is rolled down the guttering, and lands next to the object, which is then taken. The first player with three or four objects can 'sail away' to win. This game can be altered to include all sorts of curriculum targets, such as collecting objects with a certain colour, shape, letter or rhyme.
- **Beanbag darts** is another target game with a bull's-eye target and different scores in different areas. The pupil with the highest score is the winner. Letters can be placed in the circles to be collected to make words or words can be placed to make a sentence.
- **Tenpin bowls** can be played with weighted plastic bottles and heavy balls which are rolled down the guttering to knock over as many as possible. Numbers, words and curriculum pictures can be attached to the bottles. Flexible tubes can be used to roll the balls.

Balls and balloons

- **Come-back ball** can be bought commercially, or is easily made by sticking a plastic sucker onto any size ball with strong glue and attaching spiral plastic or elastic with a key ring at the other end, which is clipped to the body or part of the wheelchair.
- **Balloons** are extremely useful in games, particularly for pupils with limited muscle power.
- **Blow-up balls** are often sold to use on the beach in the summer. Pupils with fine motor difficulties find them easier to pick up when they are not fully inflated. 'Glow-in-the-dark' blow-up balls can be quite fun in a darkened room. Small bells can be put inside these balls to make the activity multi-sensory.
- **Beanbags** made from old gloves, mittens and socks can be weighted by filling a plastic bag loosely with sand or lentils, sealing the bag and stuffing it into the sock or glove.
- **Paper balls** are very lightweight and float gently through the air.

Enclosing games

Games using balls need to be contained so that balls cannot roll and be a danger to others. Use benches on their sides to make an enclosed space. Pupils in wheelchairs, will find an arm stretcher very useful as this extends and can pick up balls and beanbags out of reach. Log rolls, bought from garden centres, can be useful to contain balls, although they must be sanded down to avoid splinters.

Parachute play or play canopy is commercially produced in different sizes and suitable for children of all ages. Pupils spread the parachute out in a circle and holding the edge, raise the parachute high in the air so that it forms a mushroom shape.

Commercially-available products

There are many catalogues containing specialist equipment for pupils with disabilities, which are listed in Appendix 12. Over time schools need to build up a collection of equipment useful for many pupils. Different sizes and textures of balls and beanbags can breathe life into an old game.

Technology

Technology can be difficult for pupils with motor difficulties, because of the problems holding and using tools and utensils. Health and safety must be carefully considered when dealing with sharp tools, heat or chemicals and it is likely that an adult assistant will be required to facilitate actions for the pupil and for supervision, although with adaptations and specialist equipment pupils should be encouraged to be as independent as possible. Teachers need to be creative and practical in thinking around access problems and not be afraid to use common sense in adapting materials and equipment.

Specialist commercial equipment available

- **Adjustable-height tables, workbenches,** cookers and sinks are vital if there is more than one pupil with a disability in a school. Where there are only one or two pupils, adaptations can usually be made to meet individual needs. Vari-tech make a very strong adjustable-height table with a variety of tops such as a woodwork bench, sink, cooker and snooker table. They are easily height-adjusted by turning a handle. Other catalogues are also available.
- **Mitre saws** will hold the wood and the saw in position, so that the pupil only has to move it backwards and forwards to cut.
- **Shapersaws** are safe electric saws which cut thin wood, balsa and thick card and do not cut fingers!
- **Trolleys** can be used as walking aids and to carry objects around the room. A piece of wood placed from the trolley to the table-top means that the pupil can slide the object across, avoiding lifting its whole weight.
- **Taps** should ideally be of the lever type, but tap adaptors turn taps into lever-taps.
- **Cooker knobs** can be adapted using a device which fits over the knobs, giving a better grip.
- **Non-slip matting** prevents bowls and utensils from slipping and rolling and can be bought by the roll or as different-sized mats.
- **A spike board** holds things steady, so that they may be cut or peeled. It should be anchored on a non-slip mat.
- **Open lids** with a piece of dycem placed around the lid to give a good grip; other special devices are available to remove a variety of lids.

Geography

Understanding direction and mapping can be difficult areas for pupils with severe motor difficulties. Able-bodied children learn about distance, judgement, size of spaces, steepness of slopes and use of the appropriate language. They also learn laterality, where they are in space, and their relationship to others and objects, but a child who is not able to move around independently does not have these experiences. Many disabled children do not have any form of independent mobility until they are more than five or six years old, which affects their understanding of direction.

Practical ways to learn direction

Use directional language from an early age, while facilitating the child in moving, in the same way as you would talk to an able-bodied child. We tell young children to 'put it inside' or 'underneath' when directing them to put something away and we say 'go forwards, backwards, to the side, between the trees', when young children are learning to ride a tricycle. Because children with severe motor difficulties cannot achieve these tasks, we facilitate the actions, without verbalising them. It is important for the child to feel the movement, while hearing the appropriate language. Body awareness and direction are also learnt in therapy sessions.

- **Movement around school:** when pushing a wheelchair or buggy, movements should be verbalised, for example, 'We're going into the art room'. Ask the pupil to give directions and follow their instructions exactly. Give disabled pupils messages to deliver around the school to gain knowledge of the school layout.

- **Movement in the playground:** Groups of able-bodied and disabled pupils can take turns to direct each other through a maze chalked on the playground, into the Pharaoh's tomb or out in space amongst the stars. An adult can reflect appropriate language and mirror directional commands.

- **Computers and direction:** target and adventure games are often thought to have little value for children, but they are very good at teaching direction and mapping of the environment.

- **Maps:** any pupil with spatial or laterality difficulties will have difficulties in map reading. Maps should be enlarged and different colours used to highlight certain areas, such as high ground or rivers.

- **Virtual reality:** this is new computer technology where the player wears a visor and possibly a glove, placing the player in a three-dimensional world. There have been some exciting experiments with pupils with disabilities, enabling them to move in buildings and situations which are new to them, allowing them experiences which would otherwise be impossible. In effect, they become able-bodied. We have not quite arrived at the holo-deck on the Starship Enterprise, but we may be well on the way! This new technology is expensive and experimental at this stage, but is likely to provide great benefits for people with disabilities in the future.

- **Remote-controlled cars:** These are a very exciting way to practise controlling the direction of a vehicle and using a joystick. Early years toys often have a joystick or switch attached to the toy by a cable and because they are battery powered they can be controlled by switches via a battery adaptor.

- **Radio-controlled cars:** these are cars which do not have a cable and are controlled by radio waves via a control panel and joystick. They can be very powerful and fast and are better driven in a hall or playground. Make a 'town' or maze by chalking out the plan on the floor or using barriers. Directing and driving radio-controlled cars in this way uses map reading and teaches geographical and perceptual skills.

- **Roamer:** this is a piece of technological equipment which can be programmed to move in a specific direction and is independent of the computer or wires. It moves by keying in the direction and the distance to be travelled and does not use a joystick. The movements of the Roamer need to be planned in advance, involving quite complex thought processes in direction, distance and maths as well as spatial awareness, planning and fine motor control. The Roamer can be linked to other areas of the curriculum by creating a plan of a town, space or Victorian London. It can have card and pictures attached to turn it into an animal, coach or car.

Chapter 13

Music and art

People with physical disabilities need to be able to access music in as many different ways as possible. A hi-fi deck or television can be independently controlled by a switch. Pupils with limited arm and hand movements can have instruments attached to arms or legs using Velcro straps or they can be positioned so they can hit or shake a musical instrument with hands or feet. They need to experience a wide variety of music and develop their own taste. Adults must take care to respect another person's choice and not always impose their own taste of music in others.

*Music –
a universal
language*

Making and adapting musical instruments

It is important that children with physical disabilities hear, see and are able to touch and play real instruments as well as home-made ones.

- **Musical rope:** sew bells along a thick rope or narrow plastic tubing. Pupils sit in a line or circle holding the 'rope' playing the bells in a group.
- **Salad spinner:** bells, dried peas and various objects can be placed in a salad spinner. When the handle is turned different sounds are made.
- **Maracas:** these can be made very simply using any sealed container such as a yoghurt pot or tin. Encourage pupils to experiment with different materials to make different sounds.
- **Instrument stand:** pupils who are unable to hold an instrument may have one or more instruments mounted or hung from a stand. They may lie down, sit or stand to play the instruments. These stands are commercially available and can be attached to a wheelchair or they can be made.
- **Moos and baas:** these are small boxes which sound like animal noises when turned upside down and can be included in music, stories or songs. Fix in a large tube for an easier grip.

Electronic music

There is a bewildering array of electronic musical equipment and imaginative computer software which can operate electronic equipment by touch or sound, enabling pupils with severe and complex difficulties to compose and play their own music.

- **Soundbeam ultrasound machine** sends out an invisible beam, activated by tiny movements, creating different pitches and sounds.
- **Midi interface** enables data interchange between computers and musical keyboards via specialist software, which is accessed through the computer, to play prerecorded sounds such as any instrument or a child's voice.

- **Sound light wall** links movement of colours on a screen to changes in frequency and sound. A microphone is plugged into the unit and different visual responses are made to the variety of sounds.

Musical activities to develop fine motor control

These activities practise:
- listening skills,
- turn-taking,
- directing others,
- concentration,
- spatial awareness,
- vocalisation,
- group cooperation,
- auditory discrimination,
- anticipation,
- confidence,
- creativity,
- directionality,
- body awareness,
- memory,
- observation,
- different reactions,
- relaxing,
- self-control,
- spatial awareness,
- tactile awareness, and
- trust.

Most musical activities can be easily adapted to develop motor control by asking pupils to play instruments in various positions, e.g. up high or to the side. This might follow the pattern for high and low notes in the music or follow the words e.g. of 'The Grand Old Duke of York', and can be played while sitting, lying or standing.

- **Spinning a musical web:** a small group of pupils sit in a circle and, using a thick rope or thin plastic tubing, take turns to wind it around their arms and legs or around a doll, before passing it to the next person, while singing a song. They repeat the song and try to unwind the rope.
- **Music mat (1):** take a piece of thick material and sew on a variety of bells, musical buttons and shakers. The pupil explores the sounds independently.
- **Music mat (2):** make a music mat and cards with a picture or word of each instrument. One pupil turns over a card and directs the other to find it.
- **'Simon says':** each pupil has a musical instrument. The teacher or another pupil calls out 'Play loudly, quietly, at the side, up high, down low', but only if the direction is prefixed by the words 'Simon says'. If an instrument is played without these words, the pupil is out.

- **Orchestra:** each pupil has an instrument and they are grouped so that all the bells, drums, etc. are together in groups. Large cards are made with pictures of the instruments or words describing the instruments. The conductor has a baton (stick) with the cards placed in front, face-down. As these are turned over the conductor must point and direct the correct instruments to play along to different types of music. Another pupil can turn the cards for a pupil with motor difficulties. This is a good activity for the whole class or a small group and involves group participation, anticipation and careful observation of the conductor to play at the right time.

- **Humming:** a group of pupils sit in a circle with heads as far down to their knees as possible. They start a very quiet hum, gradually getting louder. As the hum gets louder they move their bodies upwards, ending with their arms stretched. This can be reversed, or the hum can start on a low note, gradually getting higher and louder until the climax. This practises slow and controlled movement and breath control.

- **Matching sounds:** a number of musical instruments are placed on a tray and the same instruments placed behind a screen. One pupil sits behind the screen and tries to match the instrument played on the other side. This aids memory, turn-taking, auditory discrimination, grasp and release.

- **Musical statues** can be played while sitting or standing. Pupils move their bodies while the music is playing. When it stops they must remain still or they are out. Make sure that pupils are able to keep still before playing this game and limit the time to be still to three or four seconds.

- **Musical keyboard tunes** can be played with an isolated index finger. Fix coloured stickers onto a small keyboard and write out a short, simple tune by colour or numbers on a long, thin card and place above the keyboard.

- **Musical keyboard or drum rhythms** use an isolated finger to copy rhythms on a keyboard or percussion instrument. This develops good listening skills, turn-taking and isolating fingers. Link it to the curriculum by copying the rhythm of topic words or sentences such as 'Tut-an-kha-mun' or 'Henry was born in thir-teen-eighty-seven'.

Including music in therapy

Music is ideal to include when carrying out physiotherapy stretches and therapeutic programmes requiring one-to-one out of the class. Sing a line of a song to time stretches or move, walk, throw or catch balls in time to a song. Play different background music for relaxation in the hydrotherapy or swimming pool.

Speech and language therapy and music complement each other very well. Songs and rhymes can be found or made up to cover specific aims and targets linked to the curriculum and other therapy targets. Songs might practise individual sounds at the beginning, middle or ends of words or the pupil might be asked to fill in missing words. Any activities involving movement, singing, copying, repetition and holding objects or instruments are valuable for pupils with motor difficulties.

Art   Art is widely used as a means of expressing ideas which pupils are not able to express in written form and is a valuable form of communication. Pupils become skilfull using materials and tools and creativity and imagination are encouraged. Pupils with severe motor difficulties often enjoy art and are happy to explore various mediums. It is the process of exploration of these mediums which is important and if an adult is supporting a pupil with disabilities, care must be taken not to take over and concentrate too much on the end product. An adult should only 'tidy up' a picture if asked to do so by the pupil, otherwise there is a danger that the picture becomes the adult's work. This can be quite disheartening for pupils who are proud of their achievements.

Messy activities offer sensory stimulation, which is very important, but can be difficult for pupils with tactile defensiveness. The occupational therapist can devise a programme to help these children. Tactile input contributes to many multi-sensory centres in the brain and is important to the development and functioning of the nervous system.

Using pictures to illustrate school work

Young children with disabilities are usually happy to experiment with art, but as they mature they realise that they are unable to draw representational pictures to enhance their work in the same way as their peers. It is important to make sure that they continue to experience and enjoy hands-on art using various textures, mediums and techniques, while having other means to include pictures and art in their work. It is important that pupils who are unable to draw themselves have a choice of ways of illustrating their work.

- **Colour and black and white picture libraries** are described in Chapter 10.
- **Computer graphics:** there are many graphic, clipart and drawing packages available in catalogues and local computer stores.
- **Stamps:** some software like 1st Paint uses 'stamps' with various backgrounds, making it easy to create pictures.
- **Touch screen:** for some pupils the touch screen is ideal for free and experimental drawing on the computer. Touch screens are usually attached to the front of the computer screen, but there is now a screen with a built-in touch screen for PCs only. Some touch screens need specific software to be used, while others emulate the mouse and can be used with all software.
- **Touch pad:** some laptops and portable computers have a built-in touch pad instead of a mouse, which is particularly useful for those who have weak muscles or limited movement but good finger control. They are available in large computer stores.

Practical ideas for art

- **PVA glue** can be bought in shops and from catalogues and mixed with powder paint to create a paint which will stick to smooth surfaces, thinned with water to make a glaze for plaster or clay models, or added to papier mâché to increase its strength.

- **Finger paints** can be bought in toy shops and from catalogues, but there are a number of different ways they can be made:

  1. Mix equal amounts of plain flour and powder paint with cold water.
  2. Add PVA glue and powder paint with a little water if necessary.
  3. Make up wallpaper paste (without fungicide) and mix in powder paint.
  4. Add smells to the paint by adding peppermint and massage oils.
  5. Add different textures such as rice, lentils, sand.

Put the paint on formica-topped tables, polythene sheeting, in a plastic tray, on glossy paper or card, using fingers, hands, fists, feet or elbows to make patterns. Press a piece of paper on the top to take a print. Make patterns using combs made from cardboard, forks, brushes, sticks, rollers as well as body parts.

- **Marble rolling:** use a cardboard box with low sides and cut paper to fit the base. Put marbles into small bowls of paint and take them out with a spoon, one by one, dropping them onto the paper in the box. Move the box up and down to roll the marbles creating lines and patterns. Use a separate spoon for each colour and try different-sized marbles and balls. Cat-litter trays or biscuit tins may be used for individuals. This involves using spoons, spatial awareness, tracking, cause and effect and prediction. There is no difference in outcome between the pictures produced by able-bodied children or those with disabilities.
- **Paint rollers** of different sizes and textures can be bought in DIY shops and are ideal for pupils needing to paint large areas and backgrounds. They can be held in one or two hands. The action of reaching forwards and backwards or to the sides is excellent therapy for some pupils. Using two hands turns this into a bi-lateral activity with the handle adapted into a 'T' shape.
- **Printing blocks and stamps,** rubber stamps and shaped sponges are available in local shops, covering a wide range of subjects. Pupils may find it easier to use sponges or stamps stuck onto wooden or polystyrene blocks, giving a firmer hand-hold. Make some handles big enough to use with two hands.
- **Revolving turntable:** use an old record turntable, lazy Susan or cake icer to make pictures. Paper is cut to fit the turntable and fixed to the surface. The pupil rests a paintbrush or drips paint onto the turntable, which is then revolved, making a circular pattern. Moving the brush very slightly alters the pattern. Try different colours, chalks, pastels, paint, felt-tips or a finger dipped in paint, which will strengthen and isolate the index finger. These activities are very good for people with or without disabilities.
- **Large paint brushes and paint pads** can be bought in DIY-shops and can be held with one or two hands. Pipe lagging slipped over the handles or a 'T' bar will make them easier to hold.
- **Brushes and mops:** use a wide variety of washing-up brushes and mops for painting, including nail brushes, shaving brushes, toothbrushes and make lightweight brushes by attaching pieces of foam to a dowel rod.

- **Pepperpots and flour shakers:** put dry powder paint into any pot with a pierced lid, such as a flour dredger or pepperpot, and shake it over wet paper. It will spread out on the paper creating an interesting picture. There is little difference between pictures created by disabled and able-bodied pupils.
- **Plastic deodorant bottles:** the plastic ball can be prised out, the bottle filled with thin paint and the ball replaced creating a new pen! A foam ball can be cut and the bottle pushed inside to give a larger grip.
- **Blowing paint:** drop some runny paint onto a piece of paper and using a straw or flexible tubing, blow the paint across the paper to create a picture. This activity strengthens muscles in the mouth and extends the lungs, but make sure the pupil does not suck! If they are unable to blow, use a hairdryer with adult help. The hairdryer can be started, aimed and stopped by the pupil using a switch.
- **Rubbings:** this is good scribbling practice. Stick real coins, wool, corrugated card or paper cut outs of a variety of shapes onto cardboard. Place a piece of paper over the cardboard and stick down the edges with Blu-tak. Scribble with a pencil or crayon onto the paper and the outline of the shape or texture will appear on the paper. Wallpaper with an indented pattern is also good to rub.
- **Dough:** This can be bought in most toy shops, but is expensive. It is easy to make. Dough made from 4 cups of flour, 1 cup of water and 1 to 2 cups of salt can be baked in a very slow oven (gas mark 4) for about an hour, painted when hard and varnished to create models, bowls, beads, tiles and pretend food.

Food colouring, food essences and spice powders can be added to the dough and it should keep well in a sealed container, but make sure pupils do not have any allergies. Dough is an excellent medium for pupils with motor difficulties and weak muscles. It is easy to knead, can be cut with a knife or scissors and is a good way of practising using utensils and the fine motor control needed to roll, squeeze, poke and pinch the dough. The index finger can be strengthened by poking holes in the dough and this can be linked to maths, by turning over a card with instructions to make two, four or six holes. Play with a partner to check the number of holes and record. Dough can also be rolled out with two hands (bilateral). Shapes can be cut out with cookie cutters it can be forced through a garlic press, drawn on with a variety of sticks or objects pressed into it to create a picture.

Conclusion – a careful balancing act

Every school, every teacher, every disability, every child and every parent is different and there is no perfect answer to all the questions which arise when teaching children with severe motor difficulties. I hope this book has stimulated discussions and given support, advice and strategies, which may help individual children, parents, professionals and schools. It is a book which can be 'dipped into' from time to time and may solve some problems or give some ideas to move forward. It is important to acknowledge that everyone can only do their best and that compromises may have to be made when dealing with children with such complex needs. No one professional has the answer, but the answer is more likely to be discovered when working as a team.

Education is vital for future independence in life, but so too is satisfying emotional, physical and medical needs, and a careful balancing act is required. The child must be seen as a whole person with an enormous variety of needs which may differ between home and school. We must take care to consider the family and not to overload the child with too much homework or too much therapy. By supporting the family we are supporting the child and this should always be remembered when teaching children and young people with severe motor difficulties.

Appendices

Organisations relevant to Chapter 1

Appendix 1

CSIE (Centre for Studies on Integration in Education), 415 Edgware Road, London NW2 6NB Tel: 0181 452 8642

Disability Equality in Education, 78 Mildmay Grove, London, N1 4PJ. Tel/Fax: 0171 254 3197

Integration Alliance – In Touch, 10 Norman Road, Sale, Cheshire M33 3DF Tel: 0161 962 4441

NETWORK 81 (a national network of parents with SEN, working towards inclusive education) 1—7 Woodfield Terrace, Chapel Hill, Stansted, Essex, CM24 8AJ Tel: 01279 647415

Catalogue Suppliers and other information relevant to Chapter 2

Appendix 2

Communication aids	Liberator + Easiaids + Toby Churchill
Symbol software	Widgit Software Ltd + RESOURCE

Parents in Partnership, Unit 2, Ground Floor, 70 South Lambeth Road, London SW8 1RL Tel: 0171 735 7733

Organisations relevant to Chapter 3

Appendix 3

ACE Centre (Aiding Communication in Education), Waynflete Road, Headington, Oxford OX3 8DD Tel: 01865 763508 Fax: 01865 750188 e-mail: ace-cent@dircon.co.uk

ACE/ACCESS Centre, 1 Broadbent Road, Watersheddings, Oldham OL1 4HU Tel: 0161 627 1358

CENMAC, Eltham Green Complex, 4th Floor, 1a Middle Park Avenue, Eltham, London SE9 5HL Tel: 0181 850 9229 Fax: 0181 850 9220 e-mail: cs33@cityscape.co.uk

Independent Panel for Special Education Advice (IPSEA), 22 Warren Hill Road, Woodbridge, Suffolk IP12 4DU Tel: 0161 953 7557 Fax: 0161 953 7558

Parents in Partnership, Unit 2, Ground Floor, 70 South Lambeth Road, London SW8 1RL Tel: 0171 735 7733

Catalogue suppliers relevant to Chapter 4

Appendix 4

Chairs – adjustable height	Smirthwaite + JENX
Chair and table risers	Nottingham Rehab

Floor sitters	Nottingham Rehab
Radios – two way	GLS
Standers	JENX + Taylor Therapy
Tables – adjustable height	Vari-tech + Klick + Matthews + Leckey
Toileting	Nottingham Rehab + Taylor Therapy
Tricycles – specialist	Chailey Heritage
Walkers	Nottingham Rehab + Taylor Therapy
Wheelchairs – electric	QED

Appendix 5   *Catalogue suppliers relevant to Chapter 5*

Chairs – adjustable height	Smirthwaite + JENX
Fire procedures – evac chair	PARAID
Standers	Taylor Therapy + JENX

Appendix 6   *Catalogue suppliers relevant to Chapter 6*

Balls, balloons and beanbags	Nottingham Rehab + TFH
Body parts	Nottingham Rehab + ROMPA
Chairs – adjustable height	Smirthwaite + JENX
Concept Keyboard Company	Advisory Unit: Computers in Education
Cutlery – specialist with grips	Nottingham Rehab + Smith and Nephew
Drums and tambourines	TFH + Nottingham Rehab
Finger puppets	Notingham Rehab + GLS
Grab rails	Smirthwaite + Nottingham Rehab
Inset puzzles	Nottingham Rehab + TFH
Keyboard – music	TFH + Nottingham Rehab
Magnets and boards	Nottingham Rehab + TFH
Magnet blocks	Nottingham Rehab
Musical buttons	PLANET
Musical instruments – specialist	TFH + ROMPA
Plasticene	Nottingham Rehab
Scissors – specialist	PETA UK + Nottingham Rehab
Stander	Taylor Therapy
Switches	QED + TFH + CAC
Texture games	Nottingham Rehab
Toy piano	Step By Step
Touch screen	Inclusive Technology + Lindis
Velcro (loop and hook material)	Smith and Nephew + Nottingham Rehab

Balls and beanbags	Nottingham Rehab + TFH
Body parts	Nottingham Rehab + ROMPA
Dice – various	Nottingham Rehab + ROMPA
Grips for handles and pencils	Nottingham Rehab + Chester Care
Magnetic tape – self-adhesive	Nottingham Rehab
Material which sticks to Velcro	CLIP
Non-slip matting	Chester Care + Nottingham Rehab
Pencils	Nottingham Rehab
Spoons – specialist with grips	Nottingham Rehab + Smith and Nephew
Target games	Nottingham Rehab + ROMPA
Velcro (loop and hook material)	Smith and Nephew + Nottingham Rehab

Catalogue suppliers and other information relevant to Chapter 8   ***Appendix 8***

Angleboards	Philip and Tacey + Posturite
Chairs – adjustable height	Smirthwaite + JENX
Chair risers	Nottingham Rehab
Concept keyboards	Concept Keyboard Company + Advisory Unit: Computers in Education
'Dragon dictate' software	IANSYST
Footrest – adjustable height	Smirthwaite
Headphones and splitter	Sherston Software
Head pointer	Chailey Heritage
IBM Voice Type	IANSYST
IntelliKeys	KCS, Inclusive Technology
Joysticks	CAC + SEMERC
Keyboards	KCS + Maltron
Keyguards	SEMERC + CAC
Laptop computers	RM plc + Gultronics + Toshiba
Laptray	Nottingham Rehab
Letter stickers – upper and lower case	KCS + SEMERC
Maxess tray and switch mounts	SEMERC
Non-slip matting and material	Nottingham Rehab + Chester Care
Onscreen grids – software	Crick Software + Advisory Unit: Computers in Education
Penfriend predictive software	SEMERC + Inclusive Technology

Peripherals	SEMERC + CAC
Prophet predictive software	ACE Centre (Oxford)
SEN and Switch software	Don Johnston + Inclusive Technology + SEMERC + QED + CAC
Sound files for computer	SEMERC
Symbol word processor	Widgit
Switches	QED + CAC + SEMERC
Tables and trolleys, adjustable height	Vari-tech + Leckey Designs + Klick + Matthews
Texthelp software	IANSYST + SEMERC
Touch-screen	Inclusive Technology + Lindis
Touch screen software	SEMERC
Rollerballs	Inclusive Technology + SEMERC
WiVik	ACE Centre (Oxford)
Word processor machines	TAG + NTS Computer Systems
Velcro (hook and loop material)	Nottingham Rehab + Smith and Nephew

Useful addresses

ACE Centre (Aiding Communication in Education), Waynflete Road, Headington, Oxford OX3 8DD Tel: 01865 763508 Fax: 01865 750188 e-mail: ace-cent@dircon.co.uk

ACE/ACCESS Centre, 1 Broadbent Road, Watersheddings, Oldham OL1 4HU Tel: 0161 627 1358

Advanced Rehabilitative Technologies, Sister Kenny Institute, Minneapolis, Minnesota, USA e-mail: bow@allina.com. Tim Bowman is the Project Director.

Aidis Trust, 1 Albany Park, Cabot Lane, Poole, Dorset BH17 7BX Tel: 01202 695 244. This is a charity which raises funds to provide computer systems in the home for people with severe disabilities.

The Computability Centre, PO Box 94, Birmingham Road, Warwick, CV34 5WS Tel: 0800 269 545 e-mail: tccadmin@bham.ac.uk
They provide support and training on the use of computers for people with disabilities and help match computer equipment to individuals.

The Directory of Grant Making Trusts is available from libraries and lists major national charitable trusts. Local libraries may be able to help with local charities.

The Foundation for Communication for the Disabled, Beacon House, Pyrford Road, West Byfleet, Surrey KT14 6LD Tel: 01923 336512
The foundation is a charity which can help choose the most appropriate machine and software in all parts of the UK.

NCET (National Council for Educational Technology), Milburn Hill Road, Science Park, Coventry, CV4 7JJ Tel: 01203 416994
(Web site: http://www.ncet.org.uk)

Catalogue suppliers relevant to Chapter 9

Angleboards	Philip and Tacey
Chairs – adjustable height	Smirthwaite + JENX
Foam balls	Nottingham Rehab + TFH
Grips for pencils	Nottingham Rehab
Magnet board	Nottingham Rehab
Mouldable putty to make grips	Smith and Nephew
Non-slip matting	Nottingham Rehab + Chester Care
Pencils and pens	Nottingham Rehab
Polystyrene balls	Nottingham Rehab
Scissors	Nottingham Rehab + PETA
Tables – adjustable height	Vari-tech + Leckey Designs + Klick + Matthews
Tubing to make specialist grips	Nottingham Rehab + Chester Care

Catalogue suppliers to Chapter 10

Alphabet finger puppets	Nottingham Rehab
Body-parts games	Nottingham Rehab + ROMPA
Card holder	Nottingham Rehab
Card reader and blank cards	Nottingham Rehab
Concept keyboard	Concept keyboard Company + Advisory Unit: Computers in Education
Magnetic letters and boards	TFH + Nottingham Rehab
Magnetic tape – self-adhesive	Nottingham Rehab
On-screen grids – computer software	Crick Software + Advisory Unit: Computers in Education
Reading software	SEMERC, Sherston Software
Software for computer	Inclusive technology + SEMERC + Don Johnston
Spoons with specialist handles	Nottingham Rehab + Smith and Nephew
Touch screen	Inclusive Technology + Lindis

Positive images of disabilities in books

REACH, Wellington House, Wellington Road, Wokingham, Berks. RG40 2AG Tel: 01189 891101

Letterbox Library, Unit 2, Leroy House, 436 Essex Road, London N1 3QP Tel: 0171 226 1633 Fax: 0171 226 1768

Appendix 11   *Catalogue suppliers relevant to Chapter 11*

Abacus	Nottingham Rehab + Step By Step
Aprons – large	Nottingham Rehab + ROMPA
Battery adaptors	QED + TFH
Battery-operated toys	TFH + QED
Big:Calc software	Don Johnston
Binocular microscope	GLS
Calculators	Step By Step + Philip and Tacey + GLS
Card reader	Nottingham Rehab
CCTV	Concept Systems
Chairs – adjustable height	Smirthwaite + JENX
Concept keyboard	Concept Keyboard Company + Advisory Unit: Computers in Education
Dice	Nottingham Rehab.
Electric circuit	GLS
Electric socket extender for walls	Nottingham Rehab + Chester Care
Electronic timer	GLS
Electronic thermometer	GLS
Foam to make grips	Nottingham Rehab + Chester Care
Garden tools	PETA
Hundred squares	GLS
Kettle pourer	Nottingham Rehab + Chester Care
Liquid crystal thermometer	Nottingham Rehab
Magnetic blocks, boards and numbers	Nottingham Rehab
Magnetic tape – self-adhesive	Nottingham Rehab
Magnifiers	Nottingham Rehab + GLS
Maths equipment	GLS
Non-slip matting and material	Nottingham Rehab + Chestercare
Number finger puppets	Nottingham Rehab
Number lines	Nottingham Rehab
Plasticine	Nottingham Rehab
Safety glasses and goggles	Nottingham Rehab + GLS
Sand/water trays – adjustable height	Nottingham Rehab + TFH
Scientific templates	Philip and Tacey
Sink – adjustable in height	Vari-tech
Software – maths	Don Johnston + ACE (Oxford) + Inclusive Technology
Spinner	Inclusive Technology

Table – adjustable-height	Vari-tech + Klick + Leckey Designs + Matthews
Talking digital thermometer	Chester Care
Tap turners	Nottingham Rehab + Chester Care
Velcro	Nottingham Rehab + Smith and Nephew

Catalogue suppliers and other information relevant to Chapter 12

Appendix 12

Balls and beanbags	Nottingham Rehab + TFH
Body-parts games	Nottingham Rehab + ROMPA
Compass – sylvastarter	GLS
Cookers – adjustable height	Vari-tech
Cooker knobs for easy turning	Nottingham Rehab + Chester Care
Cutlery with special handles	Nottingham Rehab + Smith and Nephew
Drill and stand	GLS
Electronic timer	Nottingham Rehab
Floor basketball	Nottingham Rehab
Fluorescent hoops and balls	TFH
Hand reacher	Nottingham Rehab
Kettle pourer	Nottingham Rehab + Chester Care
Non-slip matting	Nottingham Rehab + Chester Care
Paper balls	ROMPA
Parachute	ROMPA + Step by Step + Nottingham Rehab
Puzzle map with knobs	GLS
Roamer	GLS + REM
Scissors – specialist	Nottingham Rehab
Sensory integration activities	ROMPA
Shapersaw	Nottingham Rehab
Sinks – adjustable height	Vari-tech
Softplay	ROMPA + TFH
Spikeboard	Nottingham Rehab + Chester Care
Swimming aids	Nottingham Rehab + ROMPA
Tap adapters	Nottingham Rehab + Chester Care
Target games	Nottingham Rehab + ROMPA
Trolleys	Nottingham Rehab + Chester Care
Velcro	Nottingham Rehab + Smith and Nephew
Wheelchair rocker	ROMPA
Wobble board	Nottingham Rehab

Useful addresses

Amateur Swimming Association, Harold Fern House, Derby Square, Loughborough LE11 5AL Tel: 01509 618700 Fax: 01509 618701

British Wheelchair Sports Foundation (BWSF), Jean Stone, Harvey Road, Stoke Mandeville, Bucks HP21 9PP Tel: 01296 484848

Cerebral Palsy Sports Department (CPS), 11 Churchill Park, Colwick, Nottingham NG4 2HF Tel: 01159 401202

Disability Sports, 13 Brunswick Place, London N1 6DX Tel: 0171 490 4919

Riding for the Disabled, Avenue R, NAC Centre, Kenilworth, Warks. CV8 2LY Tel: 01203 696510 Fax: 01203 696532

London Sports Forum, Ground Floor, Leroy House, 436 Essex Road, London, N1 3QP Tel: 0171 354 8666 Fax: 0171 354 8787 Minicom: 0171 354 9554

National Association of Swimming Clubs for the Disabled, The Willows, Mayles Lane, Wickham, Hants. PO17 5ND Tel: 01329 833689

Swimming for People with Disabilities, National Co-ordinating Committee, 3 Knoll Crescent, Northwood, Middx. HA6 1HH Tel: 01923 827 142

National Wheelchair Tennis Association (NWTA), c/o The British Tennis Foundation, The Queens Club, West Kensington, London W14 9EG Tel: 0171 381 7051

Special Olympics (UK), The Otis Building, 43–59 Clapham Road, London SW9 0JZ Tel: 0171 416 7551

Appendix 13   *Catalogue suppliers relevant to Chapter 13*

Adapted musical instruments	TFH
Art pastels	Nottingham Rehab
Battery adapter	TFH
Clay, fimo and aloplast	Nottingham Rehab
Computer graphics	RESOURCE + SEMERC + Sherston Software + RM plc
Easy-hold drumsticks	TFH
Easy painter	Step By Step
Fruit shakers	Nottingham Rehab
Instrument stand	TFH
Midi interface	RM plc
Musical buttons	PLANET
Musical instruments	Nottingham Rehab + ROMPA
Music keyboards	Nottingham Rehab + TFH
Musical footmat	ROMPA
Music software	SEMERC + RM plc
Sound bean ultrasound machine	TFH + SpaceKraft
Sound light wall	ROMPA
Spoons	Nottingham Rehab + Keep Able
Sponge brushes and rollers	Nottingham Rehab + Step By Step

Switches for computer	QED + CAC
Tap-a-tune piano	Step By Step
Touch screen	Inclusive Technology + Lindis
Velcro (hook and loop material)	Nottingham Rehab + Smith and Nephew

Addresses for catalogues   *Appendix 14*

ACE Centre (Aiding Communication in Education), Waynflete Road, Headington, Oxford OX3 8DD Tel: 01865 763508 Fax: 01865 750188 e-mail: ace-cent @dircon.co.uk

Advisory Unit: Computers in Education, 126 Great North Road, Hatfield, Herts. AL9 5JZ Tel: 01707 266714 Fax: 01707 273684 Website:http://www.advisory-unit.org.uk

Cambridge Adaptive Communication (CAC), The Mount, Toft, Cambridge CB3 7RL Tel: 01223 264244 Fax: 01223 264254

CENMAC, Eltham Green Complex, 4th Floor, 1a Middle Park Avenue, Eltham, London SE9 5HL Tel: 0181 850 9229 Fax: 0181 850 9220 e-mail: cs33@cityscape.co.uk

Chailey Heritage, Rehabilitation Engineering Unit, North Chailey, Lewes, East Sussex BN8 4EF Tel: 01825 722112 Fax: 01825 723544

Chester Care, Sidings Road, Lowmoor Road Industrial Estate, Kirkby-in-Ashfield, Notts NG17 7JZ. Tel: 01623 757955 Fax: 01623 755585

CLIP, Suite 315, Business Design Centre, Upper Street, Islington, London N1 0QH. Tel: 0171 359 3643 Fax: 0171 354 4863

Computability Centre, PO Box 94, Warwick, Warks CV34 5WS Tel: (minicom) (01926) 312847 Freephone: 0800 269545 Fax: 01926 311345

Concept Keyboard Company Ltd, Moorside Road, Winnall Industrial Estate, Winchester, Hants. SO23 7RX Tel: 01962 843322 Fax: 01962 841657

Concept Systems, 204/206 Queens Road, Beeston, Nottingham NG9 2DB Tel: 0115 925 5988 Fax: 0115 925 8588

Crick Software Ltd, 1 The Avenue, Spinney Hill, Northampton NN3 6BA Tel: 01604 671691 Fax: 01604 671692 Web:http://www.cricksoft.com

Don Johnston, 18 Clarendon Court, Calver Road, Winwick Quay, Warrington WA2 8QP Tel: 01925 241642 Fax: 01925 241745

Easiaids Ltd, 5 Woodcote Park Avenue, Purley, Surrey CR8 3NH Tel/Fax: 0181 763 0203

Enabling Computer Supplies, 20 Rising Brook, Stafford, Staffs. ST17 9DB Tel/Fax : 01785 228891

GLS Fairway, 1 Mollison Avenue, Enfield EN3 7XQ Tel: 0181 805 8333

Gultronics, 217/8 Tottenham Court Road, London W1P 9AF Tel: 0171 580 9116

IANSYST Training Products, The White House, 72 Fen Road, Cambridge CB4 1UN Tel: 01223 420101 Fax: 01223 426644

Inclusive Technology, Saddleworth Business Centre, Delph, Oldham OL3 5DF Tel: 01457 819790 Fax: 01457 819799 e-mail:inclusive@inclusive.co.uk

JENX Ltd, Nutwood 28, Limestone Cottage Lane, Sheffield S6 1NJ Tel: 0114 2853376 Fax: 0114 2853528

KCS Tools for the Computer Enabled, PO Box 700, Southampton SO17 1LQ Tel: 01703 584314 Fax: 0703 584320

Keep Able, Head Office, 7 Fleming Close, Park Farm, Wellingborough, Northants NN8 6UFTel: 01933 679426

Klick Technology Ltd, Claverton Road, Wythenshawe, Manchester M23 9FT Tel: 0161 998 9726 Fax: 0161 946 0419

Leckey Designs Ltd, Kilwee Business Park, Dunmurry, N. Ireland BT17 0HD Tel: 0800 626020

Liberator, Whitegates, Swinstead, Linc. NG33 4PA Tel: 01476 550391 Fax: 01476 550357

Lindis International, Wood Farm, Linstead Magna, Halesworth, Suffolk IP19 ODU Tel: 01986 784476 Fax: 01986 785460

Maltron Ltd, 13 Orchard Lane, East Molesey, Surrey KT8 0BN Tel/Fax 0181 398 3265

Matthews Educational Furniture, PO Box 81, 61–63 Dale Street, Liverpool L69 2DN Tel: 0151 236 9851 Fax: 0151 236 8096

Nottingham Rehab, Ludlow Hill Road, West Bridgeford, Nottingham NG2 6HD Tel: 0115 945 2345 Fax: 0115 945 2124

PLANET (Play, Leisure, Advice Network), Cambridge House, Cambridge Grove, London W6 0LE Tel: 0181 741 4119 Fax: 0181 741 4505

NTS Computer Systems Ltd, Unit F11, Business and Innovations Centre, Aston Science Park, Love Lane, Birmingham B7 4BJ Tel: 0800 731 7221 Fax: 0121 687 8763

PARAID Evac+Chair, Weston Lane, Birmingham B11 3RS Tel: 0121 7066744 Fax: 0121 7066746

PETA UK, Marks Hall, Marks Hall Lane, Margaret Roading, Chelmsford, Essex CM6 1QT Tel: 01245 231118

Philip and Tacey Ltd, North Way, Andover, Hants. SP10 5BA Tel: 01264 332171

Playring Ltd, 53 Westbere Road, West Hampstead, London NW2 3SP Tel: 0171 794 9497

Posturite (UK) Ltd, PO Box 468, Halsham, East Sussex BN27 4LZ Tel: 01323 833353

QED (Quest Enabling Designs) Ltd, Ability House, 242 Gosport Road, Fareham, Hants. PO16 0SS Tel: 01329 828444 Fax: 01329 828800

REM, Great Western House, Langport, Somerset TA10 9YU Tel: 01458 253636 Fax: 01458 253646 Web:http://www.r-e-m.co.uk

REMAP, National Organiser, Eur. Ing. J.J. Wright, Hazeldene, Ightham, Kent TN15 9AD Tel: 01732 883818

RESOURCE Centre, 51 High Street, Kegworth, Derby DE74 2DA Tel: 01509 672222 Fax: 01509 672267

Rifton, Robertsbridge, East Sussex TN32 5DR Tel: 0800 387457 Fax: 01580 882250

RM plc, Research Machines, New Mill House, 183 Milton Park, Abingdon, Oxon OX14 4SE Tel: 01235 826000 Fax: 01235 826999

Rolac Ramps, Unit 6, Lawson Hunt Park, Broadbridge Heath, Horsham, West Sussex RH12 3JR. Tel: 01403 272153 Fax: 01403 272106

ROMPA, Goyt Side Road, Chesterfield, Derbyshire S40 2PH Tel: 01246 211777

SEMERC, 1 Broadbent Road, Watersheddings, Oldham OL1 4LB. Tel: 0161 6274469 Fax: 0161 6272381 email:info@semerc.demon.co.uk

Sherston Software Ltd, Angel House, Sherston, Malmesbury, Wilts.

SN16 OLH Tel: 01666 840433 Fax: 01666 840048 Website: http://www.sherston.com

Smirthwaite, 16 Wentworth Road, Heathfield, Newton Abbot, Devon TQ12 6TL Tel: 01626 835552

Smith and Nephew Homecraft Ltd, Sidings Road, Lowmoor Road Industrial Estate, Kirkby-in-Ashfield, Notts. NG17 7JZ Tel: 01623 754047 Fax: 01623 755585

SpaceKraft Ltd, Crowgill House, Rosse Street, Shipley, West Yorks. BD18 3SW Tel: 01274 581007 Fax: 01274 531966

Step By Step Ltd, Lavenham Road, Beeches Trading Estate, Yate, Bristol BS37 5QX. Tel: 01454 320200 Fax: 01454 320999

Swimfriends, PO Box 146, Chichester, West Sussex PO18 8XS Tel: 01243 789402 Fax: 01243 533414

TAG Developments Ltd, Dept SECOI, 25 Pelham Road, Gravesend, Kent DA11 0BR Tel: 01474 357350 Fax: 01474 537 887 Web:http://www.hyperstudio.com

Taylor Therapy, Woodwards Road, Walsall WS2 9RN Tel: 01922 727601 Fax: 01922 724608

TFH Fun and Achievement, 756 Barracks Road, Sandy Lane Industrial Estate, Stourport-on-Severn, Worcestershire DY13 9QB Tel: 01299 827820 Catalogue requests 01299 879360

Toby Churchill Ltd, 20 Panton Street, Cambridge, CB2 1HP Tel: 01223 576117 Fax: 01223 576118

Toshiba, PCD Marketing, PC Division, Toshiba Information Systems (UK) Ltd, Toshiba Court, Weybridge Business Park, Addlestone Road, Surrey KT15 2UL Tel: 01932 828828

Vari-tech Atkinson Engineering, Units 2,3,7, Premier Mill, Begonia Street, Darwen, Lancs. BB3 2DP Tel: 01254 773524 Fax: 01254 706617

Widgit Software Ltd, 102 Radford Road, Leamington Spa CV3 1LF Tel: 01926 885303 Fax: 01926 885293

WRK, Ashfield House, School Road, St Johns Fen End, Wisbech, Cambridgeshire PE14 7SJ Tel: 01945 880014 Fax: 01945 880910

Further useful addresses   *Appendix 15*

AFASIC (speech impairments) 347 Central Market, Smithfield, London EC1A 9NH Tel: 0171 236 3632 Fax: 0171 236 8115

Anything Left Handed, 14 Norfolk Avenue, Christchurch, Dorset BH23 2SE Tel: 01202 484013

British Computer Society Disability Group, c/o Room C126, EASAMS Ltd, West Hanningfield Road, Great Baddow, Chelmsford CMZ 8HN Tel: 01245 242 950 Fax: 01245 478317

CALL Centre (Communication Aids for Language and Learning Centre), University of Edinburgh, 4 Buccleuch Place, Edinburgh, Scotland EH8 9LW Tel: 0131 667 1438 Website: http://call-centre.cogsci.ed.ac.uk/Callhome

Contact A Family, 170 Tottenham Court Road, London W1P OHA Tel: 0171 383 3555

Council for Disabled Children, c/o National Children's Bureau, 8 Wakely Street, London EC1V 7QE Tel: 0171 278 9441

DEMAND (Design and Manufacture for Disability), Three Cedars,

Napsbury Hospital, Shenley Lane, London Colney, Herts. AL2 1AA Tel: 01727 82556 Fax: 01727 823926
Creates furniture and equipment for people with severe disabilities when no other solution exists.

Dextral Books (Left Handed Equipment), PO Box 52, South DO, Manchester M20 2PJ Tel/Fax: 0161 445 0159

Disability Equality in Education, 78 Mildmay Grove, London, N1 4PJ Tel/Fax: 0171 254 3197

Disabled Living Foundation, 380–384 Harrow Road, London W9 2HU Tel: 0171 289 6111

Hemi-Help, 166 Boundaries Road, London SW12 8HG Tel: 0181 672 3179

Independent Panel for Special Education Advice (IPSEA), 22 Warren Hill Road, Woodbridge, Suffolk IP12 4DU Tel: 0161 953 7557 Fax: 0161 953 7558

Joint Council for the GCSE, Devas Street, Manchester, M15 6EX Tel: 0161 953 7557 Fax: 0161 953 7558

MOVE International (Mobility Opportunities Via Education), University of Wolverhampton, Gorway Road, Walsall WS1 3BD Tel: 01902 323066 Fax: 01902 322858 e-mail: MOVE-Europe@compuserve.com MOVE is an exciting new programme designed to enable school staff and therapists, working as a team, to develop each pupil's independence and mobility.

National Toy Libraries Association, 66 Churchway, London NW1 1LT Tel: 0171 387 9592

NETWORK 81 (National network of parents with SEN, working towards inclusive education) 1-7 Woodfield Terrace, Chapel Hill, Stanstead, Essex CM24 8AJ Tel: 01297 647415

Parents in Partnership, Unit 2, Ground Floor, 70 South Lambeth Road, London SW8 1RL Tel: 0171 735 7733

RADAR (Royal Association for Disability and Rehabilitation), 250 City Road, London EC1 Tel: 0171 250 3222

SCOPE, Head Office, 6 Market Road, London N7 9PW Tel: 0171 6197100 Helpline: 0800 626216

SCOPE Leisure Resource Centre, 17 Clewes Road, Oakenshaw, Redditch, Hereford and Worcs., B98 7ST Tel: 01527 404808

SKILL: National Bureau for Students with Disabilities, 336 Brixton Road, London SW9 7AA Tel: 0171 2740565 Fax: 0171 737 7477

Young Minds (Information Service for Parents and Carers) Tel: 0345 626376

Bibliography

ACE Centre (1993) *Aids to Communication – Where Do I Go?* Oxford: ACE Centre.

ACE Centre (1994) *Basics to Back Technology.* Oxford: ACE Centre.

Allen, J. *et al.* (1992) *Augmentative Communication: More than Just Words.* 2nd edn. Oxford: Ace Centre.

Audit Commission/HMI (1992a) *Getting in on the Act – Provision for Pupils with Special Educational Needs. The National Perspective.* London: HMSO.

Audit Commission/HMI (1992b) *Getting the Act Together – Provision for Pupils with Special Educational Needs: A Management Handbook for School and Local Education Authorities.* London: HMSO.

Ayre, J. and Gray, C. (1995) *Seating Children for Access Technology.* Oxford: ACE Centre.

Ball, F. (1997) *The Development of Reading Skills – A Book of Resources for Teachers.* Oxford: Basil Blackwell.

Balshaw, M. H. (1991) *Help in the Classroom.* London: David Fulton Publishers.

Banes, D. and Cullen, L. (1997) 'Science for Life' in *Special Children,* February issue.

Barnes, C. (1991) *Disabled People in Britain and Discrimination.* London: Hurst.

Bean, J. and Oldfield, A. (1991) *Pied Piper – Musical Activities to Develop Basic Skills.* Cambridge: Cambridge University Press.

Brown, A. (1987) *Active Games for Children with Movement Problems.* London: Harper and Row.

Clark, C., Dyson A., Millward, A. (eds) (1995) *Towards Inclusive Schools?* London: David Fulton Publishers.

Clay, M. (1981) *The Early Detection of Reading Difficulties – A Diagnostic Survey with Recovery Procedures.* 3rd edn. Auckland: Heinemann Publishers.

Clay, M. (1993) *Reading Recovery.* Auckland: Heinemann Education.

Cocks, N. (1996) *Watch Me, I Can Do It! – Helping Children Overcome Clumsy and Uncoordinated Motor Skills.* Australia: Simon and Schuster.

Cogher, L., Savage, E., Smith, M. F. (eds) (1992) *Cerebral Palsy – The Child and the Young Person.* 2nd edn. London: Chapman and Hall.

College of Speech and Language Therapists (1992) *Schools and Speech and Language Therapy Working Together – Guidelines to Good Practice.* London.

Cotton, E. (1990) *The Hand as a Guide to Learning.* London: The Spastics Society.

Cowne, E. (1996) *The SENCO Handbook – Working within a Whole School Approach.* London: David Fulton Publishers.

Cratty, B. J. (1989) *Adapted Physical Education in the Mainstream.* Denver, CO: Love Publishing.

Denziloe, J. (1994) *Fun and Games – Practical Leisure Ideas for People with Profound Disabilities.* Oxford: Butterworth-Heinemann Ltd.

DES (1970) *Handicapped Children Act.* London: HMSO.

DES (1978) *Special Educational Needs: Report of the Committee of Enquiry into the Education of Handicapped Children and Young People* (The Warnock Report). London: HMSO.

DES (1981) *Education Act.* London:HMSO.

DfE (1993) *Education Act.* London: HMSO.

DfE (1994a) *The Code of Practice on the Identification and Assessment of Special Educational Needs.* London: HMSO.

DfE (1994b) *Special Educational Needs: A Guide for Parents.* London: HMSO.

DfE (1994c) *The Organisation of Special Educational Needs.* Circular 6/94. London: HMSO.

DfE, (1994d) *Special Educational Needs Tribunals: How to Appeal.* London: DfE Publications Centre.

DfEE, (1997) *Excellence for all Children: Meeting Special Educational Needs.* (Green Paper). London: DfEE Publications.

DHSS (1989) *The Children Act.* London: HMSO.

Dyspraxia Foundation (undated) *Praxis Makes Perfect – Recognising Developmental Coordination Disorders.* Herts: Dyspraxia Foundation.

Fagg, S. *et al.* (1992) *Entitlement for All in Practice – A Broad, Balanced and Relevant Curriculum for Pupils with Severe and Complex Learning Difficulties in the 1990s.* London: David Fulton Publishers.

Fenton, M. (1992) *Working Together Towards Independence – Guidelines for Support Staff Working with Pupils with Physical Disabilities.* London: Royal Association for Disability and Rehabilitation.

Finnie, N. (1994) *Handling the Young Cerebral Palsied Child at Home.* Oxford: Butterworth-Heinemann.

Forrester, W. and Irwin, J. (1996) *Access in London.* London: Quiller Press.

Foundation for Communication for the Disabled, (1996) *Information Technology for People with a Physical Disability.* Surrey: FCD.

Gains, C. (1994) *Collaborating to Meet Special Educational Needs.* NASEN Publications.

Gilbert, C. and Hart M. (1990) *Towards Integration – Special Needs in an Ordinary School.* London: Kogan Page.

Griffiths, M. and Clegg, M. (1998) *Cerebral Palsy: Problems and Practice.* London: Souvenir Press.

Henderson, A. (1998) *Maths for the Dyslexic.* London: David Fulton Publishers.

Hevey, D. (1992) *The Creatures Time Forgot.* London: Routledge.

Hornby, G. (1994) *Counselling in Child Disability: Skills for Working with Parents.* London: Chapman and Hall.

Housden, P. (1993) *Bucking the Market: LEAs and Special Needs.* NASEN Publications.

Jones, A. (1983) *Science for Handicapped Children.* London: Souvenir Press.

Jordan, L. and Goodey, C. (1996) *Human Rights and School Challenge – The Newham Story.* Bristol: Centre for Studies on Inclusive Education.

Jowsey, S. E. (1992) *Can I Play Too? – Physical Education for Physically*

Disabled Children In Mainstream Schools. London: David Fulton Publishers.

Kelsall, A. D. (undated) *Children with Disabilities – Equipment for the Disabled.* Oxford: The Disability Information Trust.

Kenward, H. (1996) *Spotlight on Special Educational Needs: Physical Disabilities.* NASEN Enterprises.

Kenward, H. (1997) *Integrating Pupils with Disabilities in Mainstream Schools – Making It Happen.* London: David Fulton Publishers.

Lawson, L. (1998) *Practical Record Keeping for Special Schools – Development and Resource Material for Staff working with Pupils with Special Educational Needs.* 2nd edn. London: David Fulton Publishers.

Leary, B. and Von Schneden, M. (1982) *'Simon Says' is not the Only Game.* American Foundation for the Blind.

Lee, M. and French, J. (updated) *Dyspraxia – A Handbook for Therapists.* London: The Chartered Society of Physiotherapy.

Lewis, A. (1995) *Children's Understanding of Disability.* London: Routledge.

Lowell, E. L. and Stoner, M. (1960) *Play it by Ear: Auditory Training Games.* Los Angeles, CA: John Tracey Clinic.

Male, J. (1997) *Children First: A Guide to the Needs of Disabled Children in School.* London: The Royal Society for Disability and Rehabilitation.

Masheder, M. (1989) *Let's Play Together.* London: Merlin Press Ltd.

Mason, M. (1993) *Inclusion, the Way Forward: A Guide to Integration for Young Disabled Children.* London: Voluntary Organisation Liaison Council for Under Fives.

Mason, M. and Rieser, R. (1994) *Altogether Better – from 'Special Needs' to Equality in Education.* London: Hobsons Publishing.

McNicholas, J. and McEntee, J. (1991) *Games to Improve Reading Levels.* Stafford: Nare Publications.

Meynell (1993) *Meynell Games on Parachute Play.* London: Meynell Games Publications.

Newell, P. (1988) *ACE Special Education Handbook – The Law on Children with Special Needs.* 3rd ed. London: Advisory Centre for Education.

Norwich, B. (1996) *Special Needs Education, Inclusive Education or Just Education for All?* London: Institute of Education.

Penso, D. E. (1993) *Perceptuo-Motor Difficulties – Theory and Strategies to Help Children, Adolescents and Adults.* London: Chapman and Hall.

Raymond, J. (1984) *Teaching the Child with Special Needs.* London: Ward Locke Educational.

Reason, R. and Boote, R. (1987) *Learning Difficulties in Reading and Writing: A Teacher's Manual.* 2nd edn. Berkshire: NFER-Nelson.

Reason, R. and Boote, R. (1994) *Helping Children with Reading and Spelling: A Special Needs Manual.* London: Routledge.

Rieser, R. (1995) *Invisible Children – Report of the Joint Conference on Children, Images and Disability.* London: Save the Children.

Rieser, R. and Mason, M. (1990/2) *Disability Equality in the Classroom: A Human Rights Issue.* London: Disability Equality in Education.

Ripley, K., Daines B., Barrett, J. (1997) *Dyspraxia – A Guide for Teachers and Parents.* London: David Fulton Publishers.

113

Stanton, M. (1996) *Cerebral Palsy: A Practical Guide.* London: Optima.

The Stationery Office (1997) *Excellence in Schools.* (White Paper). London.

Sugden, D. A. and Wright H. C. (1995) *Helping Your Child with Movement Difficulties.* Developmental Coordination Disorder Project, University of Leeds.

Tingle, M. (1990) *The Motor Impaired Child.* Berkshire: NFER- Nelson.

VNU Business Publications (1998) Article from *Winter 23.* Published for the British Computer Society Disability Group.

Warin, S. (1995) *Implementing the Code of Practice: Individual Education Plans.* United Kingdom: NASEN Enterprises.

Wilkinson, T. (1991) *The Death of a Child: A Book for Families.* London: Julia Macrae.